Cast On
Bind Off

Cast On
Bind Off

54 Step-by-Step Methods

LESLIE ANN BESTOR

PHOTOGRAPHY BY JOHN POLAK

Storey Publishing

The mission of Storey Publishing is to serve our customers by
publishing practical information that encourages
personal independence in harmony with the environment.

Edited by Gwen Steege and Pam Thompson
Art direction and book design by Mary Winkelman Velgos
Text production by Jennifer Jepson Smith

Photography by © John Polak
Illustrations by © Jamie Hogan

Indexed by Nancy D. Wood

Special thanks to WEBS, America's Yarn Store, for their generous donation of the Valley
Yarns Valley Superwash merino used for all the swatches

Storey Publishing
210 MASS MoCA Way
North Adams, MA 01247
www.storey.com

Printed in China by R.R. Donnelley
10 9 8 7 6 5 4

LIBRARY OF CONGRESS CATALOGING-IN-PUBLICATION DATA

Bestor, Leslie Ann.
  Cast on, bind off / by Leslie Ann Bestor.
    pages cm
  Includes index.
  ISBN 978-1-60342-724-1 (paper w/partially concealed wire-o : alk. paper)
  1. Knitting—Technique. I. Title.
TT820.B598 2012
746.432—dc23
                            2012002769

This book is for the most wonderful creation
I have ever cast on, my daughter, Cady,
and for my father, Charles,
for being a shining example of dedication
to the creative muse.

Contents

Part One

Cast Ons

Part Two

Bind Offs

Beginnings and Endings

In knitting classes at the yarn store where I work, we start beginners with a needle full of stitches already cast on, so they can begin knitting and come back to casting on when they are more comfortable with manipulating the needles and yarn.

This roughly describes my own journey with cast ons and bind offs. I learned one way and stuck with it for every single project. The Long-Tail Cast On was my friend, and since it is so versatile, I had no issues with our relationship for many years. But as I grew as a knitter and began exploring different techniques, I realized that a whole range of varied options awaited me for both starting and finishing a piece of knitting. I started to look at other ways to cast on and bind off and discovered that different situations call for different techniques, and that using the right one has a huge impact on the finished garment. The Old Norwegian Cast On became my next best friend. And I began to keep notes about which cast ons work in different situations. I carried little scraps of paper in my project bags and trawled for videos on the Internet, continually trying new ways to make my knitting match my imagination.

Most knitters progress in a similar fashion. They have a favorite cast on or bind off, and it is probably the one they learned from the person who taught them. A few workhorses, such as the Long Tail Cast On and the Traditional Bind Off, serve knitters well in many situations. But just as you learn the difference between right- and left-slanting decreases, learning new techniques for beginning and ending your projects allows you to take your knitting to a whole new level. You can choose a stretchy cast on for your top-down socks; a stable, firm beginning for the bottom of your cardigan; or a flexible bind off that allows you to block your lace shawl to its fullest. My hope is that this book opens a new world of possibilities and expands your horizons for beginning and ending a knitted project.

Use this book to learn new techniques. Keep it in your knitting bag as a reference and, with every project, try a new way to cast on and bind off. Some techniques, such as the provisional cast ons, apply to very specific situations, while others can be used for many purposes. Some of these new cast ons and bind offs you will like, some not so much. Some will be easy, some will be fiddly, but you may just find that the fiddly one is perfect for the particular piece you are working on. You will never regret investing time in the beginnings and endings of your projects: The edges set the stage for the piece as a whole. There's no point in knitting a beautifully intricate sock if its top won't stretch enough to go over your heel. With all the work we put into our knitted garments, we want all the parts to work together well.

This brings me to swatching. Of course, we all do this before beginning a project, right? Well, now you have another reason to swatch! Your swatch is the perfect place to experiment with cast ons and bind offs before you invest time in the project itself. After knitting your swatch, evaluate the edges. Are they either stretchy or firm enough for the project? Do they look good with your stitch pattern? Is the effort worth the result? Now you will be able to make choices based on many options rather than just the old standbys.

In this book you'll find 33 cast ons and 21 bind offs. Each technique features photographs illustrating every step. Check the Extras line for anything required in addition to your project needles and yarn. Having trouble? Consult the Getting It Right box, where I offer tips for refining the technique. Need suggestions for a cast on or bind off for your next project? Flip to inside the front or back cover for tips on which technique is best for which kind of project.

I hope this book becomes a trusted reference and guidebook for you. And I hope it provides some "aha" moments as you discover new methods. Maybe you, too, will find some new best friends in these techniques! Knitting is an adventure that allows us to keep learning, and my intent with this book is to encourage that ongoing exploration.

Quick Start Guide

Here are some basic techniques that will come up again and again as you try different ways of casting on and binding off. Refer back to this section when you need a refresher on these essentials.

Slip Knot

The foundation stitch for many a cast on, the slip knot is aptly named: If you pull too hard to tighten the knot (and it isn't looped around an object, such as a knitting needle), the knot *slips* apart.

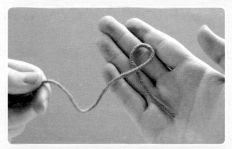

1 Make a loop with the tail end underneath the long end where the yarns overlap.

2 Reach through the loop and grab the long yarn and pull a new loop through the first loop.

3 Holding the new loop, pull on the tail to tighten just a bit. This is the loop — the slip knot — to place on your needle.

4 Pulling on the long end tightens the loop on your needle (or, if the loop is not on the needle, pulls the knot out entirely).

Overhand Knot

Another commonly used knot, the overhand joins two strands together.

1 Hold two strands of yarn with tails lined up together.

2 Make a loop and pull the ends through the loop. Tighten the knot.

Cast-On Tail

Some cast ons require you to create a long tail before you begin. This tail will be used, along with the strand of yarn going to the ball, to create the edge. There are a few different ways of measuring out the length you need:

- Measure out a length three to four times the width of your project.

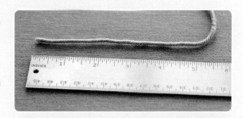

- Use approximately 1" for each stitch.

- Wrap yarn around needle 10 times and use that length to approximate 10 stitches, then measure out length needed for total number of stitches.

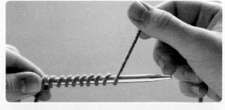

- Alternatively, for projects with a large number of stitches to cast on, use two balls of yarn. One ball provides the tail yarn; the other is the knitting yarn. Connect them with a slip knot. (Do not count knot as a cast-on stitch. Just drop it off needle at end of first row.) After casting on, drop the tail yarn and continue knitting with the other yarn.

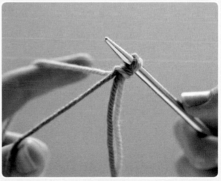

Slingshot Position

The slingshot position is used in many cast ons, so learning it is a crucial step in any knitter's education.

1 Make a slip knot and place it on the needle. Hold the needle in your right hand.

2 Let the tail yarn and ball yarn hang down. Unless otherwise instructed, the tail yarn is closest to you. Insert forefinger and thumb between the two strands of yarn hanging from the needle.

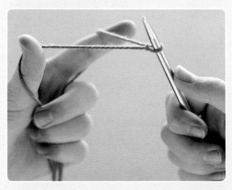

3 Use your remaining fingers to grasp the ends of the yarn in the palm of your hand and pull the yarn with your thumb and forefinger pointing up and back: The yarn looks like a slingshot.

Knitwise, Purlwise

Sometimes knitting requires you to slip a stitch from a needle without working it. Or, in the case of some of these cast ons, such as Knitted (page 31) or Cable (page 36), a newly made stitch is slipped back to the left needle. I always specify whether you should slip it knitwise or purlwise: as if to knit or as if to purl.

Knitwise: Twist the right-hand needle so the two needles are side by side and insert the tip into the new stitch from below.

Purlwise: Holding both needles so that they form a continuous line, with the tips touching, pass the stitch from one needle to the other.

Part One

Cast Ons

The beginning of a project is an exciting time, and often we are eager to jump right in and get going. You already know how important it is to knit a swatch when starting a project. And if you care about the edges of your project (and why wouldn't you?), it's also important to first consider the dozens of ways to get stitches on the needles.

Take advantage of your gauge swatch to test out some possibilities. It pays to take the time at this stage to get it right. Anything to avoid the heartache of ripping back three inches (at 100 stitches per row) because the cast on doesn't look right!

But even before swatching, start with an understanding of your project. Will the edge be ribbed or have some other stitch pattern? Does it need to stretch? A little or a lot? Will you be starting in the center and working out? Will you be coming back to add an edging later, or perhaps turning it up to make a hem?

Once you have examined your project to see what characteristics you need, look at the various cast ons to see which might fit. Look inside the front cover for a list of which ones work best in various situations. As you get to know more cast ons, you will get a good sense of your choices. Swatch, and you will discover for yourself how you like to use them.

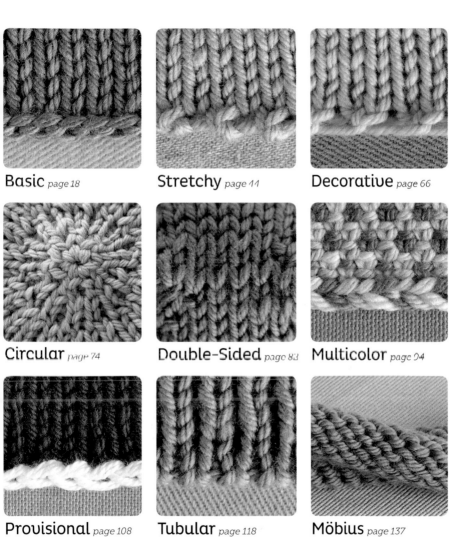

Basic *page 18*

Stretchy *page 11*

Decorative *page 66*

Circular *page 74*

Double-Sided *page 83*

Multicolor *page 94*

Provisional *page 108*

Tubular *page 118*

Möbius *page 137*

Basic Cast Ons

This first group of cast ons covers the ones most knitters learn first. In searching for a way to describe this group, I decided that "simple" was not accurate, nor did "all purpose" fit those included here. These are the basics in a knitter's wardrobe. They are some of the easiest to learn and teach, but more than that, these methods are the staples we come back to again and again for their versatility.

Invisible Ribbed Bind Off for collar (page 197)

Cable Cast On for buttonholes

Old Norwegian Cast On for the bottom edge and cuffs

Knitted Cast On at base of thumb

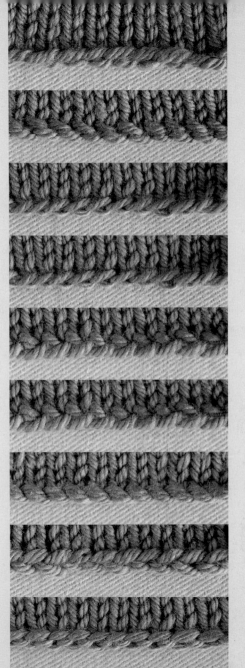

Backward Loop

Double-Twist Loop

Long-Tail

Long-Tail, Thumb Version

Knitted

Purled

Cable

Chained

Old Norwegian

Backward Loop Cast On
a.k.a. Single, Simple, Wrap

The Backward Loop Cast On is one of the simplest. Very easy to learn, it is often taught to new knitters. The sad truth, though, is that it does not produce a particularly attractive edge and does not hold up well. It also makes knitting the first row tricky. But don't discount this method altogether: the Backward Loop is one of the few cast ons that can be used to add stitches at the end of the row or in the middle of a section of stitches.

CHARACTERISTICS

- Elastic edge
- Loops between stitches can look sloppy

GOOD FOR

- Adding stitches at the ends and middles of rows, such as the underarm of a top-down sweater or base of a mitten's thumb

Working the Cast On

① Make a slip knot, leaving a short tail (approximately 4"), and place it on a needle.

② Position the working yarn (the yarn going from the needle to the ball) so that it comes from the needle in between your fingers and thumb, and then outside and around your thumb.

③ Insert the needle tip under the loop of yarn on the outside of your thumb.

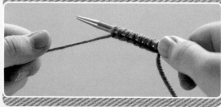

④ Let the loop slide off your thumb and gently tighten.

⑤ Repeat steps 2 and 3 for the desired number of stitches.

Double-Twist Loop Cast On

This cast on takes the Backward Loop Cast On (page 20) and adds an extra twist to it. And in doing so, it makes a firmer, more attractive edge. It is excellent for buttonholes and any place where you need to add stitches at the end of a row. My friend Nina was delighted to show me this way of casting on. I have since found it mentioned in a few books, but it is usually made with a loop that is double twisted before putting it on the needle, which I find awkward to do. Nina's method, shown to her by a friend's grandmother, is easy and very quick once you get the movements down.

CHARACTERISTICS

- Elastic, firm, attractive edge

GOOD FOR

- Buttonholes and adding stitches at the end of the row

Working the Cast On

1 Make a slip knot with a short tail and place it on the needle. Hold the needle in your right hand. If adding stitches at the end of a row, skip this and go directly to step 2.

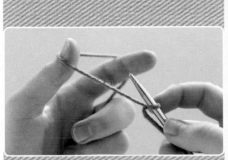

2 Wrap the working yarn so that it goes from the needle around the outside of the thumb and then around the index finger; use your other fingers to grasp the working yarn in the palm of your hand.

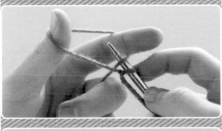

3 Insert the tip of your needle under the strand that runs from your index finger to the palm of your hand.

4 Take the needle tip over the top of the strand running between the thumb and the index finger and pull it back underneath the first strand.

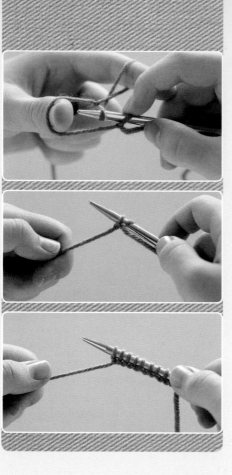

5 Rotate the needle tip to the left so that it comes up into the gap between the two strands wrapped around the thumb.

6 Drop the yarn off the thumb and index finger and gently tighten the stitch on the needle.

7 Repeat steps 2–6 for the desired number of stitches.

Long-Tail Cast On
a.k.a. Continental, Double, Two-Strand, Slingshot

This cast on is the workhorse of the many methods available. As the name suggests, you use a long tail of yarn along with the working yarn to create the cast-on edge. Fairly easy to learn, it lends itself to many different types of knitting situations. The edge it creates is firm and elastic, making it suitable for edges that will be followed by garter, stockinette, or rib stitch. It is attractive and looks good on both the front and back sides. Note that the Long-Tail Cast On, because of its structure, also creates the first row of knitting.

CHARACTERISTICS

- Edge is elastic and attractive
- First row begins with wrong (private) side of work

GOOD FOR

- Any stitch pattern and any project

Working the Cast On

① Measure out a tail of yarn using whatever method you prefer (page 13). Make a slip knot and place it on the needle.

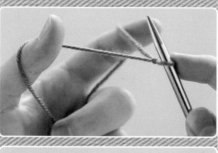

② Hold the needle in your right hand. Create a slingshot with the tail end of the yarn over your thumb and the working yarn over your index finger.

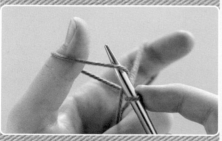

③ Using the needle, reach under and into the loop on the left thumb.

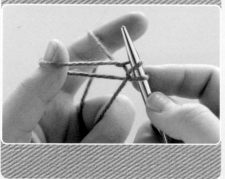

④ Go over the yarn on your left index finger and bring that yarn through the thumb loop.

5 Drop the yarn off your left thumb and gently tighten (not too tight!) the loop on the needle.

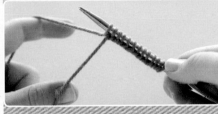

6 Repeat steps 4–6 for the desired number of stitches.

Beginning to Knit

Since this cast on makes the first row of knitting, you are ready for a wrong-side row when you begin knitting. In stockinette, for example, you work a purl row.

Getting It Right

To make the first row a little easier to work into, cast the stitches onto a needle one or two sizes larger, or even hold two needles together and cast on. For a project with many stitches to cast on, use two balls of yarn (see page 13).

Long-Tail Cast On: Thumb Version

This is a variation of the Long-Tail Cast On that is easier for some folks than holding the yarn in the traditional slingshot position. The result is the same as the standard Long-Tail Cast On.

CHARACTERISTICS

- Edge is elastic and attractive
- First row begins with wrong side (private side) of work

GOOD FOR

- Any stitch pattern and any project

Working the Cast On

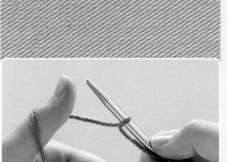

1 Measure out a tail of yarn using whatever method you prefer (page 13). Make a slip knot and place it on the needle. Hold the needle and working yarn in your right hand.

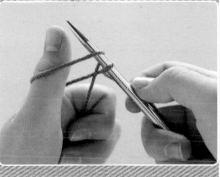

2 Wrap the tall end around your left thumb counter-clockwise (yarn comes from needle to inside thumb and wraps around to outside of thumb). Using the other fingers of your left hand to grasp the tail, insert needle tip under the thumb loop.

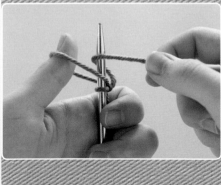

3 Holding the needle with your left hand, use your right hand to wrap the working yarn around the needle.

4 Pass thumb loop over the needle tip and pull the strand to tighten the stitch.

5 Repeat steps 2–4 for the desired number of stitches.

Knitted Cast On
a.k.a. Knitting On

This cast on is easy to remember because it is so much like a regular knit stitch, making it a common way to teach beginners. The edge, which looks good from both sides, is fairly firm, though it can stretch out of shape.

CHARACTERISTICS

- Somewhat elastic
- Easy to pull out of shape

GOOD FOR

- Beginners
- Adding stitches at ends of rows

Working the Cast On

1 Make a slip knot, leaving a short tail, and place it on a needle. Hold this needle in your left hand and an empty needle in your right hand.

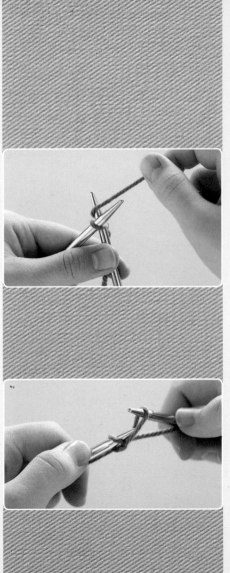

2 Insert the tip of the right-hand needle into the slip knot as if to knit, wrap the yarn around and pull through a new stitch. You probably need to hold both needles with your left hand as you wrap the yarn with your right hand.

Place this stitch on your left-hand needle. The stitch can be transferred in either of the two following ways:

3A Pass the stitch directly from the right tip to the left tip; the yarn going to the ball will be coming from the left leg of the new stitch.

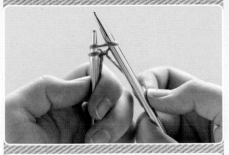

3B Twist the right-hand needle so the two needles are side by side and insert the left needle tip into the new stitch; the yarn going to the ball will be coming from the right side of the new stitch.

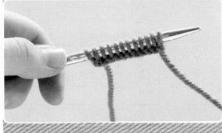

4 Continue in this manner, knitting into the last stitch on the left-hand needle and transferring the new stitch back to the left-hand needle until you have the desired number of stitches.

Getting It Right

I prefer method 3B as it adds a twist that tightens up the edge, giving it a bit more resilience. I also like it because when you finish transferring the stitch, your needle is in the correct position to cast on the next stitch. It doesn't matter which method you choose, as long as you are consistent.

To tighten up the edge, knit into the back loops on the first row of knitting.

Purled Cast On

This is a purl variation of the Knitted Cast On (page 31). The edge it produces is identical, so it works equally well in situations calling for that cast on. Some find the Purled Cast On to be faster because of the mechanics of how the stitches are created and transferred.

CHARACTERISTICS

- Somewhat elastic
- Edge can be pulled out of shape

GOOD FOR

- Beginners
- Adding stitches at ends of rows

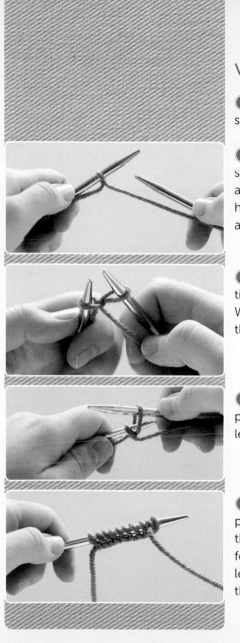

Working the Cast On

1 Make a slip knot, leaving a short tail, and place on a needle.

2 Hold the needle with the slip knot in your left hand and an empty needle in your right hand. Hold the working yarn as if you are going to knit.

3 Insert the right-hand needle tip into the slip knot as if to purl. Wrap the yarn around and pull through a new stitch.

4 Transfer the new stitch purlwise (as if to purl) to the left-hand needle.

5 Continue in this manner, purling into the last stitch on the left-hand needle and transferring the new stitch to the left-hand needle until you have the desired number of stitches.

Cable Cast On

The Cable Cast On is another knitted cast on that uses two needles. The edge is firm and not very elastic, and the appearance is neat. It is a useful cast on for adding stitches mid project because it uses just the working end of yarn. This comes in handy when adding stitches at the end of the row or when doing a one-row buttonhole. See Alternating Cable Cast On (page 49) for the ribbed version of this cast on.

CHARACTERISTICS

- Firm edge

GOOD FOR

- One-row buttonholes
- Adding stitches at ends of rows

Working the Cast On

1 Make a slip knot, leaving a short tail, and place it on the left-hand needle.

2 Knit into the slip knot, leaving the slip knot on the left-hand needle.

3 Slip the new stitch back to the left-hand needle knitwise.

4 Insert the needle between the 2 stitches on the left-hand needle and wrap yarn around.

5 Pull a new stitch through.

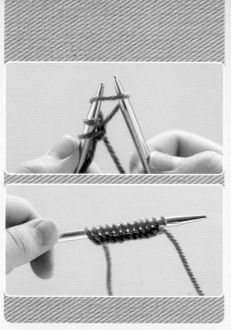

6 Slip this new stitch to the left-hand needle knitwise.

7 Continue casting on, reaching between the top 2 stitches on the left-hand needle to pull through the new stitch. Always slip that new stitch to the left-hand needle knitwise.

Getting It Right

- Work stitches loosely to facilitate inserting the needle in between the stitches.

- To neaten the last stitch: Before transferring the last stitch to the left-hand needle, pass the yarn between the needle tips to the front of the work, then slip the last stitch to the left-hand needle. This makes it neater and prevents the last stitch from slanting across the next-to-last stitch.

Chained Cast On

The Chained Cast On can be worked both as a provisional cast on and as a regular cast on. (I have included a variation in the section of provisional cast ons; see Provisional Crochet 1 Cast On, page 113). The nice thing about the Chained Cast On is that it exactly matches the Traditional Bind Off, so if you are doing a project that calls for matched ends, such as a scarf or shawl, this is the perfect cast on for it. It is neat and attractive and looks good on both sides. It is not stretchy, however, and takes some skill with a crochet hook to complete.

Extras Crochet hook (same or a size bigger than project needles)

CHARACTERISTICS

- Firm, tight edge

GOOD FOR

- Matching edges, with the Traditional Bind Off (page 148)
- Afghans and scarves

Getting It Right

If the cast-on edge pulls in, go up a size or two in the crochet hook.

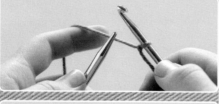

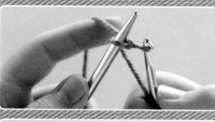

Working the Cast On

① Make a slip knot, leaving a short tail, and place it on the crochet hook.

② Holding the knitting needle in your left hand and the crochet hook in your right, bring the working yarn behind the needle.

③ Reach with the crochet hook over the top of the needle, grab a loop of yarn, and pull it through the loop on the crochet hook. This is 1 stitch.

④ Move the yarn behind the needle again.

⑤ Repeat steps 2–4 until you have one less than the desired number of stitches cast on. Slip the stitch on the crochet hook onto the needle.

Old Norwegian Cast On
a.k.a. Twisted German, Elastic Long-Tail

This cast on is a variation of the Long-Tail Cast On (page 25). It is, however, much more elastic, making it suitable for socks and other pieces that need a very stretchy edge. After years of using the Long-Tail as my go-to cast on, I discovered the Old Norwegian, and it became my new best friend. I love the extra elasticity it adds, without losing any neatness.

CHARACTERISTICS

- Very elastic
- Neat edge

GOOD FOR

- Any stitch pattern and any project
- Cuffs of socks, mittens, gloves, and hats

Working the Cast On

1 Make a slip knot, leaving a long tail (page 13). Place it on a needle and hold yarn in the slingshot position.

2 Insert the needle tip under both strands of the tail yarn on your thumb.

3 Come over the top and down into the thumb loop, coming out underneath the strand that is in front of your thumb.

4 Bend your left thumb toward the index finger and reach over the top of the strand on your index finger. The loop on your thumb now has an X in it.

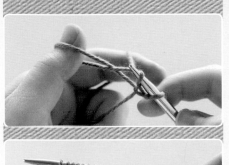

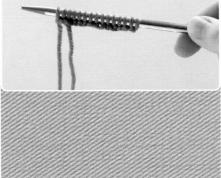

5 Bring the needle tip through the bottom half of the X (nearest the needle), grab the index finger yarn to make your new stitch, drop the thumb loop, and tighten stitch.

6 Repeat steps 2–5 for the desired number of stitches.

Beginning to Knit

As with the Long-Tail Cast On (page 25), this technique creates the first row of knitting with the cast on. This means that for stockinette fabric, your first row will be a purl row.

Getting It Right

You may need to go up a needle size to prevent an edge that is too tight.

Stretchy Cast Ons

Most of these cast ons create an edge that consists of knits and purls in combination: the natural start for any ribbing. A couple of exceptions to this (Slip Knot, Tillybuddy's) are included here because their great elasticity makes them well suited to garments that need a stretchy edge, such as socks, mittens, gloves, and hats. These cast ons have the advantage of looking good on both sides, allowing you to begin with either a right-side or wrong-side row. Although this group works well with ribbed edges, many of the techniques can be used with stockinette as well (see photos on pages 52, 56, and 59 for examples).

Sewn Bind Off for neck (page 195)

Tillybuddy's Very Stretchy Cast On for cuffs

Channel Island Cast On for bottom of sweater

Alternating Long-Tail Cast On

This variation of the Long-Tail Cast On (page 25) can be used for pieces that start with ribbing. It has the same elastic properties as the Long-Tail and makes a neat edge. You can use it to create any pattern of ribbing by alternating the knit and purl cast-on stitches as needed.

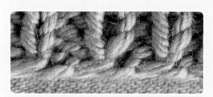

CHARACTERISTICS

- Neat edge; looks good on both sides
- Moderately elastic edge

GOOD FOR

- Any ribbing (K1, P1; K2, P2; K1, P3; and so on)

Getting It Right

You may need to go up a needle size to prevent an edge that is too tight.

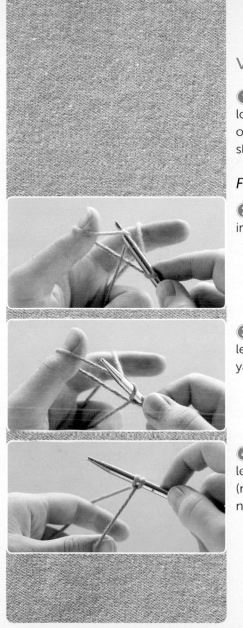

Working the Cast On

① Make a slip knot, leaving a long tail (page 13), and place it on the needle. Hold yarn in the slingshot position.

For a Knit Stitch

② Reach the needle under and into the loop on the left thumb.

③ Go over the yarn on your left forefinger and bring that yarn through the thumb loop.

④ Drop the yarn off your left thumb and gently tighten (not too tight!) the loop on the needle.

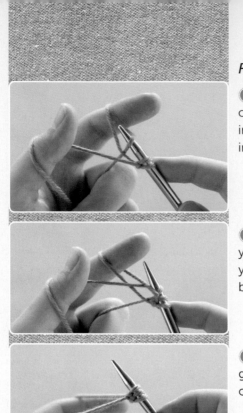

For a Purl Stitch

5 Reach the needle to the outside of the index finger and insert it from underneath up into the finger loop.

6 Reach the needle under the yarn coming from the needle to your thumb and pull that yarn back through the finger loop.

7 Drop the yarn off your finger and gently tighten the loop on the needle.

8 Alternate casting on knit and purl stitches as required for your ribbing, for the desired number of stitches.

Alternating Cable Cast On

This is a variation of the Cable Cast On (page 36) that incorporates purl stitches, making it suitable for ribbed edges. The edge is neat and firm and not too stretchy. It would be useful for ribbed edges where you want a neat edge that doesn't require a lot of give, such as the bottom edge of a cardigan. Directions are for K1, P1 rib, but you can use them for any rib pattern by following the order of knits and purls called for in the rib.

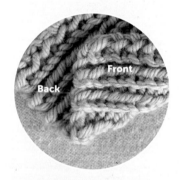

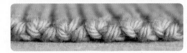

CHARACTERISTICS

- Neat edge for ribbing; looks good on both sides
- Firm edge

GOOD FOR

- Any ribbing (K1, P1; K2, P2; K1, P3; and so on)

Working the Cast On

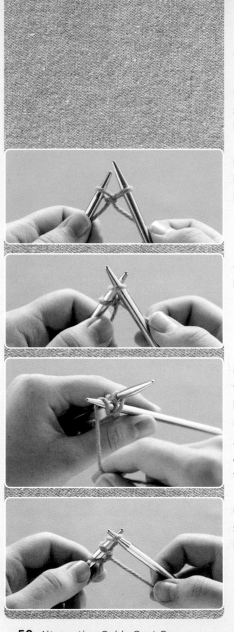

1 Make a slip knot, leaving a short tail, and place it on the left-hand needle.

2 Knit into the slip knot, leaving the slip knot on the left-hand needle.

3 Slip the new stitch to the left-hand needle knitwise.

4 Bring the yarn around to the front. Reaching behind the left-hand needle, insert the right-hand needle between the 2 stitches, wrap the yarn around as if to purl and pull the stitch through.

5 Slip this new stitch (a purl stitch) to the left-hand needle knitwise.

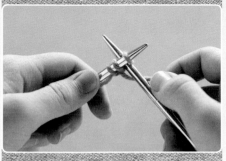

6 Bring the yarn to the back. From the front, insert the right-hand needle between the end-most 2 stitches, wrap the yarn around, and pull the new stitch through. Slip this new stitch (a knit stitch) to the left-hand needle knitwise.

7 Continue in this manner, alternating knit and purl stitches until you have the desired number of stitches cast on. The new stitch is always made by going between the 2 stitches closest to the tip of the left-hand needle.

Getting It Right

- Work stitches loosely to facilitate inserting the needle in between the stitches.

- To neaten the last stitch: Before transferring the last stitch to the left-hand needle, pass the yarn between the needle tips to the front of the work then slip the last stitch to the left-hand needle. This makes it neater and prevents the last stitch from slanting across the next-to-last stitch.

Double Start Cast On

a.k.a. Estonian, Latvian

This cast on is very stretchy and creates a good base for K1, P1 and K2, P2 ribbing. Because of this, it is often used for the cuffs of socks, mittens, and hats. It is like the Long-Tail Cast On (page 25) in construction; the difference is in the second stitch of each cast-on pair, where the yarn wraps in the reverse direction around the thumb. Nancy Bush suggests adding an extra strand or two of yarn on the thumb side to make a more pronounced and decorative edge.

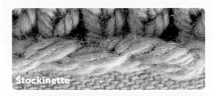
Stockinette

Stockinette

CHARACTERISTICS

- Stretchy edge
- Decorative edge

GOOD FOR

- Tops of socks
- Cuffs that call for a slightly more pronounced edge

Ribbed

Ribbed

Working the Cast On

1 Make a slip knot, leaving a long tail (page 13), and place it on the needle. Hold the yarn and needle in the slingshot position.

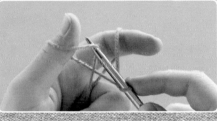

2 Reach with the needle under and into the loop on the left thumb.

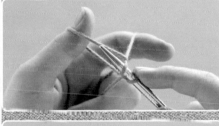

3 Go over the yarn on your left forefinger and bring that yarn through the thumb loop.

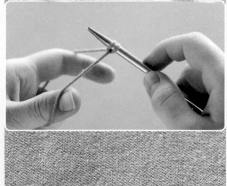

4 Drop the yarn off your left thumb and gently tighten (not too tight!) the loop on the needle. (So far, this is the same as Long-Tail Cast On).

5 Reposition the yarn on your thumb so that the yarn comes from the needle to the outside of the thumb and wraps to the inside across the palm of the hand.

6 Insert needle tip under the yarn coming from the thumb across the palm of the hand.

7 Reach over the top of the finger yarn, and bring that yarn through the thumb loop.

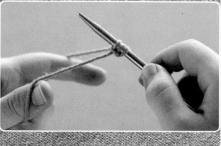

8 Drop the yarn off your thumb and gently tighten the loop on the needle.

⑨ Repeat steps 2–8 for the desired number of stitches.

Getting It Right

The edge can be made more pronounced by increasing the number of strands of yarn going to the thumb. To do this with one extra strand, measure out a length for the tail that is double what is needed for cast on. Fold this in half and make a slip knot where the two strands come together (see step 1, page 57). Hold the yarns in slingshot position, with the doubled strand going over the thumb.

Channel Island Cast On
a.k.a. Knotted

This cast on produces a strong, elastic edge with a series of bumps or knots, almost like picots. The flexibility makes it suited for top-down socks, while the decorative edge adds a nice bit of interest to edges of garments. Knitted ganseys often use this cast on, and because it is made with an extra strand of yarn, it holds up well. This technique makes an even number of stitches.

Stockinette

Stockinette

CHARACTERISTICS

- Decorative edge
- Stretchy edge
- Strong and long-wearing edge

Ribbed

GOOD FOR

- Bottom edge of sweaters
- Cuffs
- Gansey sweaters

Ribbed

Working the Cast On

1 Measure out a tail that is twice the length you would need for a Long-Tail Cast On. Fold this in half and make a slip knot where the two strands come together, leaving a short tail for weaving in later. Place the slipknot on your needle.

2 Hold the yarn in slingshot position, with the single strand (the one connected to the ball of yarn) going over your index finger. Take the double-strand tail and loop it, counterclockwise, twice around your thumb.

3 Reach the needle behind the single strand of yarn, as if making a yarnover.

4 Insert the needle tip up under the two doubled tails on the thumb.

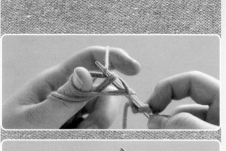

5 Reach over the top of the single strand and pull a loop through.

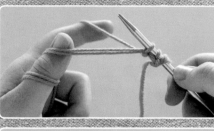

6 Drop the yarn from your thumb and pull on the ends to snug the stitch.

7 Repeat steps 2–6 for the desired number of stitches. Note that this sequence makes 2 stitches: the first a yarnover and the second a knot.

Getting It Right

On the first row of knitting, knit the knots and purl the yarnovers. At the end of the first row, treat the two strands of the slip knot as 2 stitches. This creates an even number of stitches. For an odd number of stitches you may use the slip knot as 1 stitch (though this can be rather bulky) or decrease/increase 1 stitch in the first row of knitting.

Slip Knot Cast On

a.k.a. Buttonhole, Jeny's Stretchy Slip Knot

This cast on is simply a string of slip knots lined up on your needle. It creates a very elastic edge that is great for the tops of socks, the ribbing on sleeve cuffs and mittens, and other places where you want a lot of stretch. When followed by ribbing, the cast-on edge looks great — it makes neat little accordion folds that follow the stitches. On stockinette, however, the edge looks unfinished, and I would reserve its use for edges that will be seamed. Additionally, it is great for adding on stitches at the end of rows.

Stockinette

Stockinette

CHARACTERISTICS

- Very stretchy edge
- Neat in appearance when followed by ribbing

Ribbed

GOOD FOR

- Adding stitches at end of row
- Buttonholes
- Any very stretchy ribbed edges

Ribbed

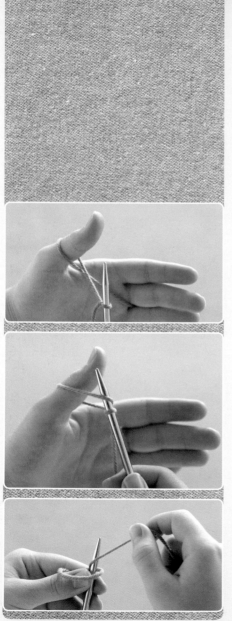

Working the Cast On

1 Make a slip knot, leaving a short tail, and place it on your needle. (If you are casting on at the end of the row, skip this and start with step 2.)

2 With the working end of the yarn, make a loop around your left thumb. The yarn goes from the needle, between the thumb and forefinger, and wraps around the outside of the thumb, with the working end of the yarn then going underneath and to the right of the needle.

3 Insert the tip of the needle into the thumb loop.

4 With your right hand, wrap the working yarn around the needle tip as if to knit.

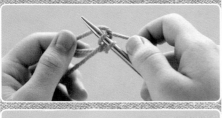

5 Pass the thumb loop over the tip of the needle.

6 Tighten stitch on needle. (See Getting It Right, below.)

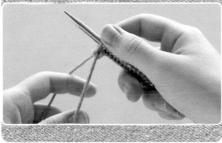

7 Repeat steps 2–6 for the desired number of stitches.

Getting It Right

It is important to get the stitches snugged up tight against each other. Use your right thumb and forefinger to hold the loop in place on the needle while pulling with your left hand to tighten the stitch. You want to avoid slack yarn between the cast-on stitches. Even though it may seem tight with the stitches snugged against each other, the finished edge will actually be quite stretchy.

Tillybuddy's Very Stretchy Cast On

for Double and Single Ribbing

This unusual cast on creates a very elastic edge, making a wonderful foundation for ribbed edges needing stretch. A variation of the Lace Cast On (page 67), it is the brain child of Jane Pimlott, who is known as Tillybuddy on Ravelry, the online knitting community. Jane was looking for a stretchy cast on that was more stable to knit on the first row than a loop cast on. She played with yarnovers and twisting the needles until she came up with this wonderful technique. The edge follows the zigzag line of the rib stitches and springs back to shape beautifully.

Front
Back

K1, P1 Ribbing

K1, P1 Ribbing

K2, P2 Ribbing

K2, P2 Ribbing

CHARACTERISTICS

- Very stretchy edge

GOOD FOR

- K1, P1 or K2, P2 ribbing
- Socks, hats, and more

Working the Cast On

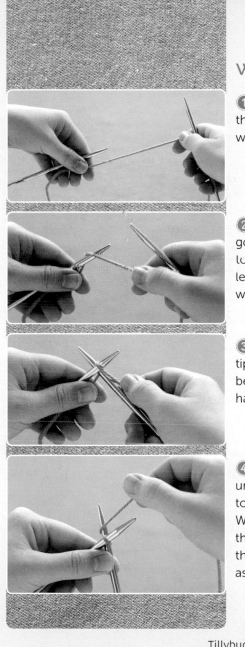

1 Hold the yarn parallel to the horizontal left-hand needle, with the tail on the left.

2 Wrap the yarn so that it goes under, behind, over the top, and back to the front of the left-hand needle. Hold the tail with your left hand.

3 Insert the right-hand needle tip to the left of the wrap, between the yarn and the left-hand needle, from front to back.

4 Bring the yarn around, under the left-hand needle, and to the back of both needles. Wrap the yarn around the tip of the right-hand needle and pull the loop through to the front, as if knitting a stitch.

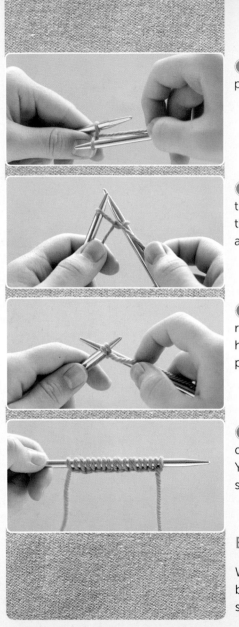

5 Your needle tips are now pointing in opposite directions.

6 Swing the right-hand needle tip under the working yarn so that it faces the same direction as the left-hand needle.

7 Transfer the stitch on the right-hand needle to the left-hand needle, from tip to tip, purlwise.

8 Repeat steps 2–7 for the desired number of stitches. You are casting on in pairs of stitches.

Beginning to Knit

When starting to knit, always begin the first row with a knit stitch.

Getting It Right

On the first row work close to the needle tips. This prevents a gap between the pairs of stitches.

Lace
page 67

Picot
page 70

Decorative
Cast Ons

Sometimes you want a little something special for your cast-on edge. One way to do that is to go back and add a knitted or crocheted trim later, but why not add pizzazz *while* you cast on? These next cast ons create edges with loops or picots, sparks of interest to liven up your knitting.

Picot 2 Bind Off for neck and armholes (page 188)

Picot Cast On for bottom edge of sweater dress

Lace Cast On for edge of blanket

Lace Cast On

The Lace Cast On is a simple cast on that creates decorative loops along the edge. It would be useful for edges where you will be picking up stitches later or tying on fringe. By itself, it tends to curl unless you follow it with rows of garter, ribbing, moss, or seed stitch that help it to lie flat. Note that the sequence described produces two stitches.

CHARACTERISTICS

- Stretchy edge
- Decorative loops on edge

GOOD FOR

- Lace
- Casting on an odd number of stitches
- Edges where you want to add fringe
- Edges you want to pick up later

Working the Cast On

1 Make a slip knot, leaving a short tail, and place it on the left-hand needle.

2 Wrap the working yarn from back to front, over the top of the left-hand needle, to make a yarnover.

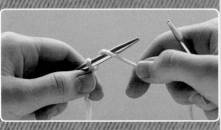

3 Insert the right-hand needle between the slip knot and the yarnover, in between the needle and the yarn under it.

4 Wrap the yarn around the needle and pull through a loop.

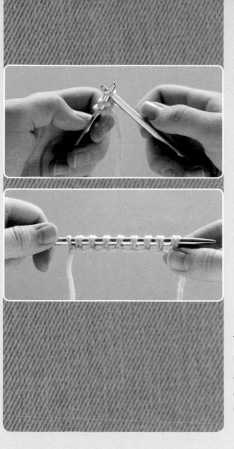

5 Transfer the new stitch from the right-hand needle to the left-hand needle knitwise.

6 Repeat steps 2–5 until the desired number of stitches is cast on.

Beginning to Knit

This method creates an uneven number of stitches. If you need an even number of stitches, drop the slip knot off the needle when you work the first row.

Picot Cast On

The Picot Cast On is used to make a decorative edge with little points, or picots, along it. It's great for when you want a little textural accent along your cast-on edge. It's also fairly stretchy, and I know people who swear by it for casting on top-down socks. This cast on is a combination of the Knitted Cast On (page 31) and picots, which are made by casting on and then binding off extra stitches along the edge. This cast on matches the Picot 1 Bind Off.

CHARACTERISTICS

- Decorative edge
- Stretchy edge

GOOD FOR

- Tops of socks
- Lace
- Any edge where you want both stretch and decorative interest
- Matching the Picot 1 Bind Off (page 185)

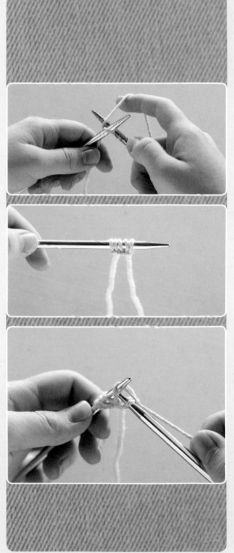

Working the Cast On

① Make a slip knot, leaving a short tail, and place on the left-hand needle.

② Insert the right-hand needle tip into the slip knot, wrap the yarn around, and pull the new stitch through. Place this stitch on the left-hand needle knitwise.

③ Continue in this manner and cast on 3 more stitches for a total of 5 stitches.

④ Knit the first 2 stitches, pull the first stitch over the second and off the right-hand needle: This binds off 1 stitch.

Knit the next stitch and bind it off by pulling the first stitch on the right-hand needle over the second.

5 Pass the remaining stitch on the right-hand needle back to the left-hand needle.

6 Using the Knitted Cast On (page 31) cast on 4 more stitches.

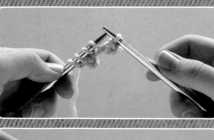

7 Knit and bind off the first 2 stitches.

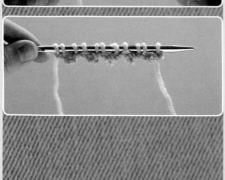

8 Repeat steps 6 and 7 until you have cast on the desired number of stitches. This creates one picot for every 3 stitches you cast on.

Variations

You can vary the distance between picots by casting on more stitches between the bind-off points.

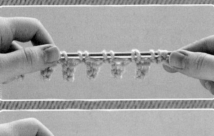

You can also vary the size of your picots by casting on and binding off more . . .

or fewer stitches.

Getting It Right

To tighten up the edge, work with a needle one or two sizes smaller than the pattern calls for.

Circular Cast Ons

This section is devoted to cast-on methods that begin at the center of a piece. Although it is possible to cast on a specified number of stitches and join them into a round, that creates a hole in the middle, which you may not want. The cast ons described on the following pages provide the means to begin in the middle without that hole or gap. In both techniques you cast on over a loop of yarn and then pull the tail to tighten the loop after you have knit a few rounds.

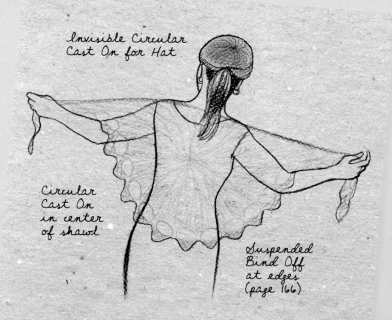

Invisible Circular
Cast On for Hat

Circular
Cast On
in center
of shawl

Suspended
Bind Off
at edges
(page 166)

Circular
page 76

Invisible Circular
page 79

Circular Cast On
a.k.a. Emily Ocker's Cast On

This cast on is used for pieces that are started in the center and worked out, such as circular shawls, hats, and mittens worked from the tip down, as well as bowls or other rounded vessels. The center is nearly invisible because you can tighten it with the tail. This is a great cast on to use in patterns that call for you to cast on four to eight stitches and work out from there.

Extras Crochet hook (same size as project needle); blunt tapestry needle

CHARACTERISTICS

- Leaves no hole at center of cast on
- A little bulkier than the Invisible Circular Cast On

GOOD FOR

- Circular shawls and blankets
- Top-down hats
- Bags

Back

Front

Working the Cast On

1 Loop the yarn so that the working yarn is on top and the tail is underneath (the tail will be going to the left).

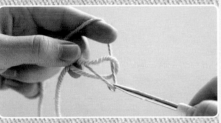

2 Using a crochet hook, reach through the loop, wrap the working yarn around the hook and pull it through the loop. Do not tighten up the loop.

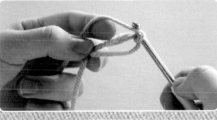

3 Wrap the yarn around the hook again.

4 Pull it through the loop already on the hook. Yes, this is a single crochet. Leave it on the hook.

5 Repeat steps 2–4. Now you have 2 stitches.

6 Continue in this manner, reaching the hook through the big loop, pulling through a loop and then wrapping and pulling through to make a single cro-chet, until you have the desired number of stitches.

Beginning to Knit

7 Slide the stitches off the crochet hook, one at a time, onto double-point or circular needles to begin knitting in the round.

8 After a couple of rows pull on the tail to close the center hole. Weave in the tail to secure the end.

Invisible Circular Cast On

This cast on is a great way to begin projects worked from the center out, such as circular lace shawls, blankets, and throws. It also works well for hats worked from the top down. The tail functions as a drawstring to pull in the center loop. In structure, it is like a provisional cast on done over a loop of yarn.

Extras Blunt tapestry needle

CHARACTERISTICS

- Invisible beginning with no hole
- Less bulky than the Circular Cast On

GOOD FOR

- Circular shawls and blankets
- Top-down hats
- Bags

Back

Front

Working the Cast On

Note: This casts on an odd number of stitches. If you need an even number of stitches, see Getting It Right.

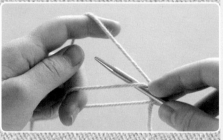

1 Make a loop of yarn, with the working yarn on top and going to the left. The tail will be underneath and on the right. This is the loop you're going to use while casting on all your stitches.

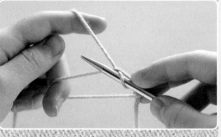

2 Reach the needle through the loop from the front and catch the working yarn and pull it through. (But don't tighten the loop; keep going.)

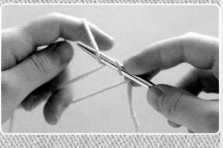

3 Reach over the top of the loop and catch the working yarn (like a yarnover) to create the second stitch.

4 Repeat steps 2 and 3 until you have one less than the desired number of stitches. Work step 2 once more.

⑤ Transfer the stitches to double-point needles (or circular needles if using either the Magic Loop or two-circulars method).

Beginning to Knit

⑥ Join stitches into a round, being careful to not twist stitches, and then begin knitting.

Tighten the cast-on loop by pulling the tail. This hole tends to work itself open as you knit. You can tighten it again when you've completed your project, and then secure it by weaving in the end.

Getting It Right

- If you need an even number of stitches, make one more yarnover before joining into a round.

- When starting to knit, join the stitches into a round; otherwise, the cast-on row will look like purl bumps (although that could be a nice design element).

Double-Sided
Cast Ons

The next section of cast ons presents techniques that are most commonly used for toe-up socks. They can be used, though, for any piece that starts with an enclosed end, such as the bottoms of bags and top-down hats or mittens. The construction of these cast ons creates two rows of stitches that are connected in the middle, allowing you to knit a tubelike piece with no hole in the center.

   Although all of these double-sided cast ons can be worked on the double-point needles you'll most likely be using for your project, it is easiest to cast on with two same-size circular needles. (It's okay if they are different lengths; they just need to be the same diameter.) The benefit of circular needles is that after casting on you can slide the lower stitches onto the cable of the needle where they stay out of the way while you work on the upper stitches. This makes these cast ons considerably easier to maneuver.

Judy's Magic
page 84

Turkish
page 87

Figure 8
page 90

Turkish Cast On at the bottom of the bag

Jeny's Surprisingly Stretchy Bind Off for top of socks (page 174)

Judy's Magic Cast On at the toe

Judy's Magic Cast On

This wonderful cast on is the invention of Judy Becker, who generously gave me permission to include it here. It is a way to cast on for an enclosed object, such as the toe of a sock or the bottom of a bag – invisibly! Therein lies the magic. I also find it neater than the Turkish and Figure 8 cast ons. It is possible to start this cast on with a slip knot on the top needle, though I've found that little knot bothers some people; it can be a bit looser than the surrounding stitches. But if it makes it easier or less confusing for you, go ahead and use a slip knot instead of wrapping the yarn as described here.

Extras Two same-size circular needles

CHARACTERISTICS

- Neat "edge"
- Invisible on both sides
- No gap between first rows of knitting

GOOD FOR

- Toe-up socks
- Bags
- Top-down hats and mittens

Working the Cast On

1 Hold the two needles together with your right hand, tips pointing left.

2 Loop the yarn around the top needle, with the tail sandwiched between the top needle and the bottom needle and coming out the back. The tail should have approximately ¾" for each stitch you are casting on. The working yarn will go over the top needle.

3 Pick up the yarns with your left hand in the slingshot position, with the tail over your index finger and the working yarn over your thumb. This twists the yarns and creates a loop on the top needle that counts as the first stitch.

4 While holding the stitch in place with a finger on your right hand, rotate the pair of needles up and wrap the yarn on your finger around the bottom needle, as if making a yarnover. Gently tighten the loop.

Judy's Magic Cast On **85**

⑤ Rotate the pair of needles downward and wrap the thumb yarn around the top needle as if making a yarnover. Gently tighten the loop.

⑥ Repeat steps 4 and 5 to cast on the desired number of stitches. Alternate between top and bottom needles, with thumb yarn wrapping around top needle and finger yarn wrapping around bottom needle. End with step 4.

Beginning to Knit

⑦ Turn the needles so that the bottom one is on top and the yarn ends on the right. Drop the tail and bring the working yarn up behind the top needle. Make sure the tail lies under the working yarn, between it and the needle. This twists the yarns so you can knit the first stitch. Knit the first row. The first stitch may become a little loose; just pull on the tail to tighten it.

⑧ Turn needles at end of first row and knit the next row (the second half of the first round).

Turkish Cast On

a.k.a. Middle Eastern

The Turkish is probably the easiest of the double-sided cast ons to learn and remember, because you are just wrapping yarn around the needles. And precisely because you are just wrapping around both needles, it tends to get a bit loose and is harder to maintain even, neat stitches.

Extras Two same-size circular needles

CHARACTERISTICS

- Invisible beginning
- Can be a little loose and sloppy

GOOD FOR

- Toe-up socks
- Bags
- Top-down hats and mittens

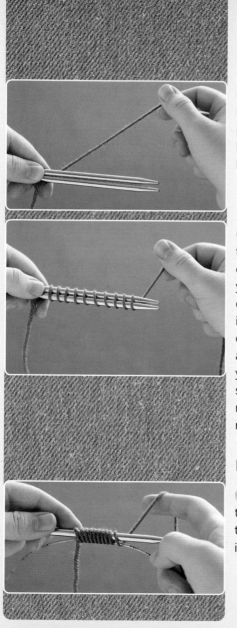

Working the Cast On

1 Hold needles parallel in your left hand with the needle tips pointing right and the yarn held behind the needles, with the tail hanging down in the back.

2 Working left to right, wrap the yarn around both needles counterclockwise. Wrap the yarn half as many times as the desired number of stitches (that is, if the pattern calls for casting on 20 stitches, wrap it 10 times around the needles). End with yarn behind the needles. Make sure that you have an equal number of wraps around each needle.

Beginning to Knit

3 Pull the bottom needle so that the bottom loops are on the cable of the needle, allowing the tips to dangle.

④ Knit across the stitches on the top needle.

⑤ Rotate your work so the bottom needle is now on top and turn to knit across the needle. Slide the loops of the top needle to the tip so they are ready to knit; slide the bottom stitches onto the cable of that needle.

⑥ Knit across the stitches on the top needle. If you want to switch to double-point needles, do so after the first row or two of knitting.

Getting It Right

This cast on can also be started with a slip knot to hold the yarn in place. To begin, make a slip knot and place it on the bottom needle. Then wrap the yarn as in step 2. When you reach the slip knot on the first round of knitting, just slip it off the needle without knitting it.

Figure 8 Cast On

The Figure 8 Cast On is easier to learn and commit to memory than Judy's Magic (page 84). It makes a serviceable beginning for socks, though it can be tricky to keep it tight and neat. It also creates a slight gap in the center between the first two rows of knitting.

Extras Two same-size circular needles

CHARACTERISTICS

- Invisible beginning
- Can be loose and sloppy

GOOD FOR

- Beginners
- Toe-up socks
- Bags
- Top-down hats and mittens

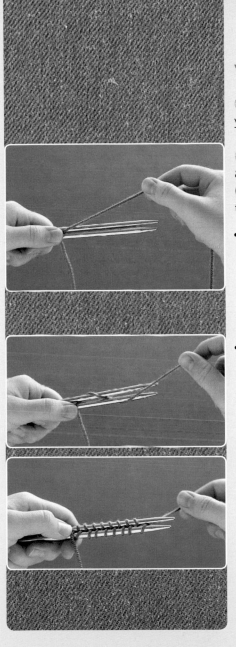

Working the Cast On

1 Hold two needles parallel in your left hand.

2 Wrap the yarn in a figure 8 around the needles as follows. (Note that you work from left to right.)

- Leaving a short (6") tail, hold it against the front of the bottom needle and bring the working yarn between the needles, behind, and over the top needle.

- Now bring the yarn from above the top needle, between the needles to the back, and wrap down and under the bottom needle, and back to the front again.

3 Continue wrapping a figure 8 around the needles until you have the desired number of stitches cast on. The yarn always goes between the needles from front to back. End with a bottom loop: You will have an equal number of stitches on top and bottom needles.

Figure 8 Cast On **91**

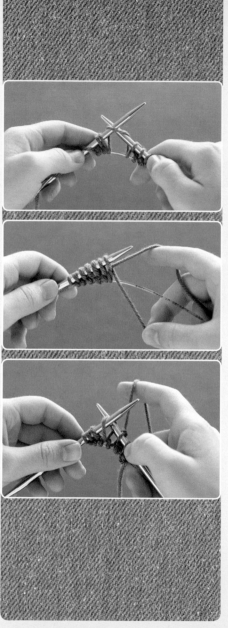

Beginning to Knit

④ Pull the bottom needle so that the bottom loops are on the cable of the needle, allowing the tips to dangle. Knit across the stitches on the top needle.

⑤ Rotate your work so the bottom needle is now on top and turn to knit across the needle. Slide the loops of the top needle to the tip, ready to knit; slide the bottom stitches onto the cable of that needle.

⑥ Knit into the backs of the stitches on the top needle (just for this first round).

Getting It Right

After you complete the first round, you can tighten stitches on the cast-on row by inserting a needle tip into the purl bumps of the first row and giving a little pull. Continue knitting as called for in the pattern.

Figure 8 Cast On **93**

Multicolor
Cast Ons

These types of cast ons have their origins in Fair Isle, Latvian, and other multicolored knitting traditions. They require a bit more work, but the end results are well worth it. The first two techniques produce a braided edge, where the colors wrap around each other. The Twined Cast On has a solid, contrast-color edge that can be paired with two other colors in the first row. Because these techniques are based on some basic cast-on methods (Long-Tail for the Braided cast ons and Twisted German for the Twined), they are relatively easy to learn. The tricky part is keeping the yarns organized and untangled. I find it easiest to keep the balls of yarn lying separately on each side of me and rotate the balls as I switch yarn positions. Alternatively, you can untangle the yarns in stages as you work the cast on.

All of these cast ons work the first row of knitting as part of the cast on. This means you will be starting a wrong-side row if knitting flat. If knitting in the round, you will join the round and commence with your first right-side row.

Two-Color Braided
page 96

Tricolor Braided
page 100

Twined
page 103

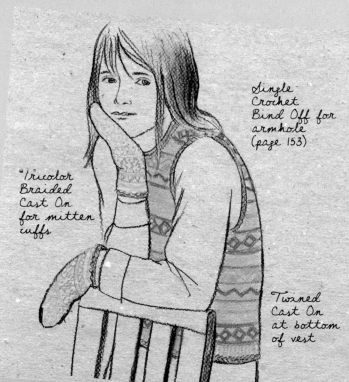

Single Crochet Bind Off for armhole (page 153)

Tricolor Braided Cast On for mitten cuffs

Twined Cast On at bottom of vest

Two-Color Braided Cast On

This braided cast on is a decorative method using two yarn colors. It produces a firm, attractive edge with a good amount of stretch. This method is slow to work, but the end result is worth it, especially when used in combination with two-color stitch patterns, such as the corrugated ribbing shown below. I see this as a beautiful edge, for instance, around the bottom of a colorwork mitten. In structure, this cast on is like the Long-Tail Cast On (page 25), but using two colors of yarn.

Corrugated

Corrugated

CHARACTERISTICS

- Attractive multicolor edge
- Elastic edge

GOOD FOR

- Corrugated, or two-color, ribbing
- Bottoms of mittens and hats
- Stranded knitting, such as that in Fair Isle or Scandinavian patterns
- Any multicolor knitting: helix, mosaic, twined, and more

This cast-on method produces two unique edges, depending on which way you twist the yarn.

A counterclockwise twist makes an edge that looks like a cord. This is the way to set up the corrugated ribbing too.

A clockwise twist gives the edge a braided look.

Working the Cast On

1 Holding the two yarns together, make a slip knot, leaving a short tail, and place it on the needle.

2 Hold the yarn in slingshot position, with yarn A (in this example, maroon) going over the thumb and yarn B (orange) going over the index finger.

3 Make the first stitch as in Long-Tail Cast On (page 25): Reach up under the thumb yarn, grab the finger yarn, and pull a stitch through. Pull the yarn snug around the needle.

Note: For a simple contrast edge, continue in this manner across the cast-on edge. Yarn A (maroon) forms the border and yarn B (orange) is ready to knit the body of your garment.

Getting It Right

The slip knot can be used as the first stitch, though it's bulkier than the other stitches. Alternatively, it can be dropped off the needle after knitting the first row.

Switch the position of the yarns before making the next stitch. This is what determines the finished look of the cast-on edge.

4A *For cord:* Move yarn B (orange) from the finger *over* yarn A (maroon) and wrap it around the thumb. Move yarn A (maroon) back to the index finger, making sure it goes under yarn B (orange). This twists the yarns in a counterclockwise direction.

4B *For braid:* Move yarn B (orange) from the finger *under* yarn A (maroon) and wrap it around the thumb. Move yarn A (maroon) back to the index finger, making sure it goes over yarn B (orange). This twists the yarns in a clockwise direction.

5 Continue casting on, switching the position of yarns between each stitch.

Tricolor Braided Cast On

Another variation of the Long-Tail Cast On, this highly decorative cast on creates a fun and beautiful edge. It lends itself to ethnic patterns, such as Latvian knitting, that involve complex colorwork. It is slow going and rather fiddly, but the resulting edge is stunning. Three colors are typically used; you can try more, but this creates longer floats that may snag, so you probably don't want to use more than four or five colors.

CHARACTERISTICS

- Beautiful multicolor edge
- Elastic edge

GOOD FOR

- Bottoms of mittens and hats
- Any multicolor knitting projects with more than two colors

Getting It Right

This can be worked using more colors of yarn; just follow the clockwise rotation. Because each additional color adds more float length, make sure the floaters are not so long that they create snagging hazards.

Working the Cast On

1 Make a slip knot, leaving short tails, with all three colors of yarn (A, B, and C) and place it on the needle. This does not count as a stitch.

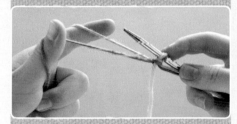

2 Hold yarn A (teal) over the thumb, yarn B (aqua) over the finger as for the Two-Color Braided Cast On; let yarn C (light green) hang down and out of the way.

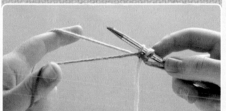

3 Make a stitch as in Long-Tail Cast On (page 25), pull to snug the stitch on the needle as usual, but leave it on the loose side so the cast on does not become too tight.

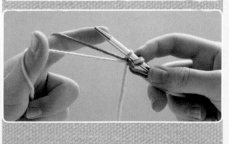

4 Rotate yarns: Drop yarn B (aqua) to the back, move yarn A (teal) to the finger, and bring yarn C (light green) to the thumb.

5 Make another stitch.

6 Rotate yarns: Drop yarn on finger, move thumb yarn to finger, and move yarn that has been dangling (not used in last stitch) to the thumb.

7 Continue in this manner, making stitches and rotating yarns, until you have the desired number of stitches. You will see that the yarns are rotating clockwise.

Swatch

This sample of tricolor linen stitch shows the particular importance of swatching in multicolor knitting. All swatches in this book have been cast on and knitted with size 8 needles.

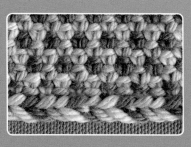

For this one, though, I had to switch to a *size 4* needle for the casting on, because the many slipped stitches of linen stitch make for such a tight fabric. And still that lovely cast-on edge looks a bit larger than the body of the knitted fabric.

Twined Cast On

This unique cast on also can be done with two or three colors, creating a striking edge for colorwork garments. Worked in two colors, the edge is a decorative contrast to the knitted garment and creates an interesting braided effect. With three colors, you get the contrasting edge and alternating colors in the first row, making it the perfect setup for corrugated, or two-color, ribbing. In structure, the cast on is like the Old Norwegian Cast On (page 41), but using multiple colors of yarn. It differs from the other multicolor cast ons in that the thumb yarn remains the same throughout, forming the single-color contrast edge.

CHARACTERISTICS

- Distinctive, colorful edge
- Elastic edge

GOOD FOR

- Corrugated, or two-color, ribbing
- Bottoms of mittens and hats
- Any multicolor knitting: stranded, helix, mosaic, twined, and more

Before You Begin

Decide how many colors (one, two, or three) you want to be part of your twined edge. To work in two colors as pictured on the previous page, yarn A (light blue) is the contrast color and yarn B and yarn C are both lavender.

If you want to set up two-color ribbing, as pictured here, yarn A (navy) is the contrast color, and yarn B (light blue) and yarn C (lavender) set up the body of the fabric.

Or, three strands of the same color yarn create a beautiful textured edge.

Working the Cast On

1 With all three yarns and leaving short tails, make a slip knot and place on the needle. The slip knot does not count as a stitch.

2 Hold the yarns in the sling-shot position, with yarn A (this is the color that forms the contrast edge; in this case, navy) going to the thumb and yarn B (light blue) going to the index finger. Allow yarn C (lavender) to just hang out of the way at the back. Yarn A (navy) is always on the thumb; yarns B (light blue) and C (lavender) alternate on the finger.

3 Insert the needle tip under both strands of yarn on your thumb.

4 Bring the needle over the top and down into the thumb loop, coming out underneath the strand that is in front of your thumb.

5 Bend your left thumb toward the index finger and reach over the top of the strand on your index finger.

6 The loop on your thumb now has an X in it. Bring the needle tip through the bottom (nearest the needle) of the X.

7 Drop the thumb loop and tighten the stitch.

8 Drop yarn B (light blue) to the front and bring yarn C (lavender) up behind it, holding yarn C over the index finger.

9 Repeat steps 3–8, always dropping one color yarn to the front and bringing the new color yarn up behind it. The thumb yarn always stays the same.

Beginning to Knit

Remove the slip knot when working the first row of knitting. Your first row of knitting will be a wrong-side row if working flat. If knitting in the round, join stitches and begin with the first right-side row.

Provisional
Cast Ons

A provisional cast on is a temporary cast on. It is worked so that the cast-on stitches can be removed later and the live stitches placed on a needle to be knit. The cast on is done with waste yarn — a smooth, slippery yarn, often in a contrasting color, that can be easily removed. It is a useful cast on for knitting hems and for edges where you want to add a border or knit in the opposite direction later. It is ideal for scarves when you want both ends to be identical: Start with a provisional cast on at what will be the center of the scarf, knit half, and then go back and remove the cast on and work the second half of the scarf to match the first.

One thing that should be noted about provisional cast ons is that the stitches are actually formed by the loops *between* the upper stitches, and thus are one-half stitch off from the stitches going upward. This doesn't matter if you are knitting stockinette or ribbing. If you plan, however, to continue a color or texture pattern, the stitches will be offset from each other. You can get around this by working a few rows of another stitch or adding a contrasting color stripe before working down.

Provisional
page 110

Provisional Crochet 1
page 113

Provisional Crochet 2
page 116

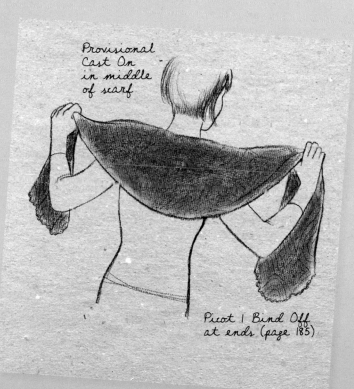

Provisional
Cast On
in middle
of scarf

Picot 1 Bind Off
at ends (page 185)

Provisional Cast On

This method has you cast on stitches around a piece of waste yarn. The waste yarn is never knit; it merely serves as a base to hold the cast-on stitches together. I find it easiest to use a contrasting color of waste yarn so I can tell the two yarns apart. But I love this method the most because of this tip: Instead of using waste yarn, I use the cable of a circular needle to cast on, and when I am ready to knit the second half, the stitches are already on the needle, so I don't have to pull anything out!

Extras Waste yarn; circular needle (optional)

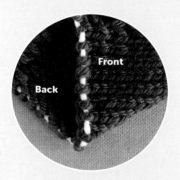

CHARACTERISTICS

- Provisional edge
- Easiest provisional method if you have a circular needle

GOOD FOR

- Adding a border or I-cord
- Working in the opposite direction later
- Hems

Working the Cast On

1 Knot the working yarn together with the waste yarn in an overhand knot (page 12). Hold the knot and needle in your right hand, using the index finger to hold the knot against the needle.

2 Hold the waste yarn over your left thumb, and the working yarn over your index finger in the slingshot position.

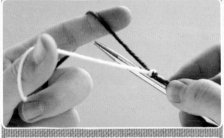

3 Reach under the waste yarn, over the top of the working yarn, and bring the working yarn under and in front of waste yarn. This is 1 stitch.

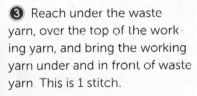

4 Reach over the top of the waste yarn and behind the working yarn, pulling it forward (like doing a yarnover). This is your second stitch.

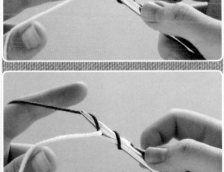

5 Repeat steps 3 and 4 until you have the desired number of stitches cast on. If you need to cast on an even number of stitches, start with step 4 (yarnover step). Note that the waste yarn only loops through the bottom of the stitches. All the stitches are made with the working yarn, ready to be knit.

Picking up the Live Stitches

Later, when you're ready to knit in the opposite direction or add a border, pull the waste yarn out and place the live stitches on a needle.

Getting It Right

To use a circular needle instead of waste yarn, skip steps 1 and 2 and instead make a slip knot with the working yarn and slide it onto the cable of a circular needle, using your right index finger to hold the knot in place. Hold the yarn over your left index finger and the cable of the needle between your thumb and middle finger. Proceed with step 3, substituting "cable" for "waste yarn." When you are ready to knit in the opposite direction, your needle is already in place.

Provisional Crochet 1 Cast On

a.k.a. Provisional Chained

This is essentially the same cast on as the Chained Cast On (page 39). The difference here is that you use waste yarn for the cast-on edge and remove it later, when you are ready to work on those stitches again. If you are proficient with a crochet hook, this can be a very fast cast on.

Extras Crochet hook in a size equivalent to the knitting needle size required for the project; waste yarn

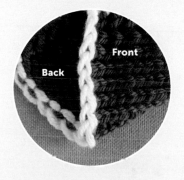
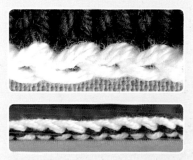

CHARACTERISTICS

- Provisional edge

GOOD FOR

- Crocheters
- Adding a border or I-cord
- Working in the opposite direction later
- Hems

Working the Cast On

1 Make a slip knot with the waste yarn and place it on the crochet hook. (This does not count as a stitch.)

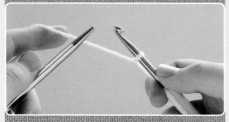

2 Holding the knitting needle in your left hand and the crochet hook in your right hand, bring the yarn behind the needle.

3 Reach with the crochet hook over the top of the needle, grab a loop of yarn, and pull it through the loop on the crochet hook. This is 1 stitch.

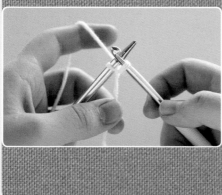

4 Move the yarn behind the needle again.

5 Repeat steps 3 and 4 until you have cast on the required number of stitches.

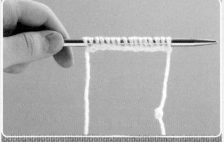

6 Cut the yarn and pull through the last stitch. Tie a knot in the end of this yarn so you know which end to unravel from.

Beginning to Knit

7 Knit with your working yarn into the stitches you've cast on with the waste yarn.

Picking Up Live Stitches

When you are ready to knit from the cast-on edge, undo the knotted tail end of the crochet chain and gently pull the chain out, slipping the live stitches onto a needle. I do this slowly, a few stitches at a time, transferring the open stitches onto my knitting needle.

Provisional Crochet 2 Cast On

This is another way of doing a Provisional Crochet Cast On. You begin by crocheting a chain, usually with more stitches than you need to cast on. You then knit into the bumps on the back of the crochet chain. It can be tricky to locate the bumps in the back of the chain, but if your chain is long enough it won't matter if you miss a few.

Extras Smooth waste yarn; crochet hook one or two sizes larger than the knitting needle size required for the project

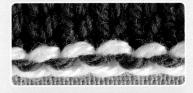

CHARACTERISTICS

- Provisional edge
- Easy to remove waste yarn
- Can be tricky to find bumps on back of chain

GOOD FOR

- Crocheters
- Adding a border or I-cord
- Working in the opposite direction later
- Hems

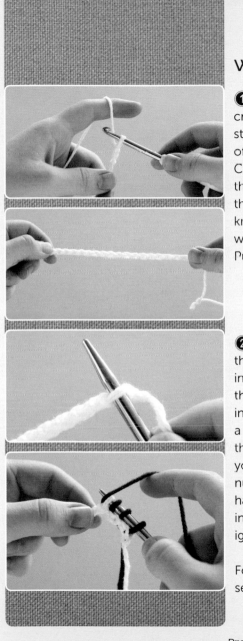

Working the Cast On

1 Using smooth waste yarn, crochet a chain that is several stitches longer than the number of stitches you need to cast on. Cut the yarn and pull it through the last loop. Make a knot on the end of this yarn so that you know which end to start with when pulling the chain out later. Put the crochet hook aside.

2 Turn the chain over. Insert the tip of your knitting needle into the bump on the back of the first chain. Wrap your working yarn around the tip and pull a stitch through. Repeat across the back of the chain until you have cast on the desired number of stitches. You may have extra crochet chain hanging down at the end; if so, just ignore it.

For how to pick up live stitches, see the box on page 115.

Tubular Cast Ons

Tubular cast ons create an edge that appears to have no beginning to it; the stitches seem to just roll over the edge. They are extremely elastic in construction and are frequently used for ribbed edges, making them useful for hats, gloves, mittens, socks, and sweater cuffs that need a lot of stretch. They are called "tubular" because the first few rows create a tube of knitting, with the knits and purls separated into front and back. This is accomplished by knitting every other stitch and slipping the ones in between, making two layers of fabric.

The needle size for tubular cast ons can be a little tricky. Many people recommend needles a size or two smaller than used for your ribbing to keep the bottom from flaring out. You want to make sure, though, that you don't tighten it up so much that you compromise the elasticity these cast ons are known for. My preference is to use the size needles called for in the ribbing. As with all new techniques, a little swatching will give you the answer.

The instructions in this section are for K1, P1 ribbing, but they can be easily modified for other ribbing patterns. The directions for creating K2, P2 ribbing at the end of this chapter (see page 135) are applicable to any of these cast ons.

Tubular

Provisional Tubular

Yarnover Tubular

Italian Tubular

Tubular
Cast On

Tubular Cast On

This edge starts with half the number of stitches needed cast on in waste yarn followed by four rows in stockinette in the main yarn color. You then increase by picking up stitches from your first row of main color knitting; this creates the tubular edge.

Extras Waste yarn

CHARACTERISTICS

- Stretchy edge
- Edge looks rolled over, seemingly without beginning

GOOD FOR

- K1, P1 ribbing
- Hats, gloves, mittens, socks, and cuffs

Working the Cast On

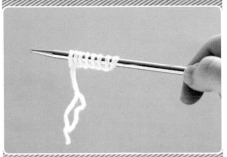

1 Using waste yarn and your choice of cast on method, cast on half the number of stitches you need. Cut the waste yarn. Work 4 rows stockinette in the main color: purl 1 row, knit 1 row, and repeat these 2 rows once more.

2 On the next row, purl the first stitch.

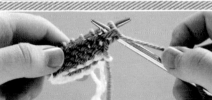

3 Reach the tip of the right-hand needle from top to bottom through the first purl bump of the main color yarn in the first row of main-color knitting 4 rows below.

4 Lift that stitch up and place it on the left-hand needle. Knit this stitch.

5 Purl the next stitch.

6 Repeat steps 3–5 across the row.

Beginning to Knit

Work K1, P1 ribbing as established (knit the knits and purl the purls). This is the first row of knitting. After several rows, snip and pull out the waste yarn.

Getting It Right

- Make sure your waste yarn is smooth and easy to pull out.

- Picking up the purl bumps can be a bit tricky, but if you have used a contrasting color for the waste yarn, you should be able to see them clearly.

Provisional Tubular Cast On

This method begins with the Provisional Cast On (page 110) before starting the tubular rows. If you are already comfortable with the concept of provisional cast ons, this can be the easiest method to use for a tubular cast on. This is my favorite of the tubular cast ons, because I love the provisional base that starts it. I also like not having to pick up stitches (as in the previous Tubular Cast On) or do yarn overs (as in the next Yarnover Tubular Cast On). This cast on matches the Tubular Bind Off.

CHARACTERISTICS

- Stretchy edge
- Edge looks rolled over, seemingly without beginning
- Bulky yarn causes edges to flare out

GOOD FOR

- K1, P1 or K2, P2 ribbing
- Matching the Tubular Bind Off (page 200)
- Hats, gloves, mittens, socks, and cuffs

Working the Cast On

Note: This cast on makes an odd number of stitches. For an even number, after step 1, skip to step 3 and then repeat steps 2 and 3 until the desired stitches are cast on. Instead of working steps 6 and 7, work only step 6 a total of four times before beginning a regular rib stitch.

1 Knot the working yarn and the waste yarn together in an overhand knot. Hold the knot and needle in your right hand, using your index finger to hold the knot against the needle. With your left hand, hold the yarn in slingshot position, with the waste yarn over your left thumb and the working yarn over your index finger.

2 Reach under the waste yarn, over the top of working yarn and bring the working yarn under and in front of waste yarn. This is 1 stitch.

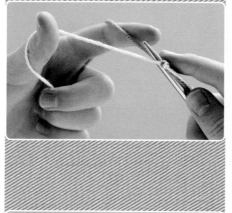

3 Reach over the top of waste yarn and scoop the working yarn forward (like doing a yarnover). This is your second stitch.

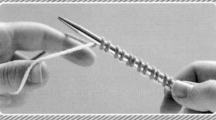

4 Repeat steps 2 and 3 until you have cast on one fewer than the desired number of stitches. Work step 2 once more: You should have an odd number of stitches.

5 All the stitches are made with the working yarn. The waste yarn loops through the bottom of the stitches. Up to this point the cast on has been like the Provisional Cast On. Now, turn work and drop the waste yarn.

6 With the working yarn, *K1, with yarn in front slip 1 stitch purlwise, move yarn to back; repeat from * across row.

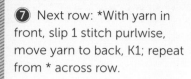

7 Next row: *With yarn in front, slip 1 stitch purlwise, move yarn to back, K1; repeat from * across row.

8 Repeat steps 6 and 7 once more (a total of 4 rows worked).

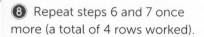

Beginning to Knit

Begin working K1, P1 ribbing. After a few rows, pull waste yarn out of the beginning row. You may have to snip it every couple of stitches and pick it out of the edge.

Getting It Right

- Use a needle size suitable for ribbing, usually one or two sizes smaller than needles used for garment, for this cast on.

- Make sure your waste yarn is smooth and easy to pull out.

Yarnover Tubular Cast On

This tubular cast on begins with a Chained Cast On (page 39) in half the number of stitches needed. The remaining stitches are then added with yarnovers, followed by tubular knitting and then ribbing. It is an excellent choice for working in the round and for K2, P2 as well as K1, P1 ribbing. Because of the yarnovers, using a needle two sizes smaller than the ribbing can keep the edge from flaring out. Swatch to see how it works for you.

Extras Waste yarn; crochet hook; knitting needles two sizes smaller than required for the ribbing

CHARACTERISTICS

- Stretchy edge
- Edge looks rolled over, seemingly without beginning

GOOD FOR

- Working in the round
- K1, P1 or K2, P2 ribbing
- Hats, gloves, mittens, socks, and cuffs

Working the Cast On

① Using waste yarn and needles in a size appropriate for ribbing, cast on half the number of stitches using a Chained Cast On (page 39). Cut yarn. With main color yarn and needles two sizes smaller than ribbing needle, work as follows.

Note: For working in the round, proceed to the bottom of page 130. For working an odd number of stitches in rows, proceed to page 130. For working an even number of stitches, keep going!

Working in Rows/Even
② K2, *yo, K1; repeat from * across.

3 *K1, slip next stitch purlwise with yarn in front; repeat from * across.

4 Repeat step 3 for three more rows.

5 *K1, P1; repeat from * across. Change to needles used for ribbing. Repeat this row until ribbing is the desired length. Remove waste yarn.

Getting It Right

Working an odd number of stitches in a row involves all the same moves shown above — yarnovers, purlwise slipped stitches, and knits — but in a different order and number (see next page).

Getting It Right

It is important to pull tightly on the end stitches when working in rows. This keeps the stitches from getting too loose, especially in rows with an odd number of stitches where you are slipping the first stitch on some rows.

Working in Rows/Odd

2 K1, *yo, K1; repeat from * across.

3 K1, *slip next stitch purlwise with yarn in front, K1; repeat from * across.

4 With yarn in front, slip first stitch purlwise, *K1, slip next stitch purlwise with yarn in front; repeat from * across.

5 Repeat step 3.

6 Repeat step 4.

7 K1, *P1, K1; repeat from * across.

8 Change to needles used for ribbing. P1, *K1, P1; repeat from * across.

9 Repeat steps 7 and 8 until ribbing is the desired length. Remove waste yarn.

Working in Rounds

2 *K1, yo; repeat from * to end. Join into a round, being careful not to twist stitches.

3 *K1, slip next stitch purlwise with yarn in front; repeat from * around.

4 *With yarn in back, slip next stitch purlwise, move yarn to front and purl the next stitch; repeat from * around.

5 Repeat step 3.

6 Repeat step 4.

7 *K1, P1, repeat from * around. Change to needles used for ribbing. Repeat this round until ribbing is the desired length. Remove waste yarn.

Italian Tubular Cast On

This tubular cast on appears to be like the Provisional Cast On (page 110), but in fact it is not the same, so be careful when making the stitches. Some people use smaller needles through the tubular knit rows to avoid a loose edge, but you want the edge to be stretchy, so make sure to swatch if you are thinking of decreasing the needle size. This cast on does not use waste yarn; just begin with your knitting yarn. Many people love this cast on for its simplicity; it's nice not to mess with pulling out waste yarn.

Extras Smaller needle size than used for rest of project (optional)

CHARACTERISTICS

- Stretchy edge
- Edge looks rolled over, seemingly without beginning
- No waste yarn to pull out
- Difficult to keep stitches from twisting on a circular needle

GOOD FOR

- K1, P1 or K2, P2 ribbing
- Matching the Tubular Bind Off (page 200)
- Hats, gloves, mittens, socks, and cuffs

Working the Cast On

1 Make a slip knot, with a tail that is four times in length what you are casting on. Place the slip knot on the needle and hold the needle in your right hand. Hold yarn in your left hand in the slingshot position (page 14), with the tail over the thumb and the working yarn over the index finger.

2 Reach the needle tip over the top of the working yarn (over your index finger), down underneath, then over the top of the tail (thumb yarn) and pull the loop back up behind and to the top of the working yarn. This stitch has a bump at the base and resembles a purl stitch.

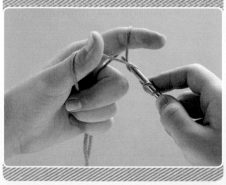

3 Reach the needle tip in front of and then under the tail (thumb) yarn, over the top of the working yarn, and pull the loop forward underneath the tail yarn and back up to the top. This stitch is smooth on the bottom and resembles a knit stitch.

4 Repeat steps 3 and 4 for the desired number of stitches. The last stitch will be unsecured and treated in one of two ways: Twist the yarns around each other before working the next row, or make the last stitch as if doing a Long-Tail Cast On (page 25). This creates a half hitch that secures the yarns.

5 You now work 2 or 4 rows of tubular knitting. For tubular knitting, you knit the knit stitches and slip the purl stitches purl-wise with the yarn in front. For the first row only, knit into the backs of the knit stitches. (This keeps the stitches from twisting.) If the last stitch was cast on as in step 3, the first stitch of row 1 will be a knit. If the last stitch was cast on as in step 4, the first stitch of row 1 will be slipped purlwise with yarn in front.

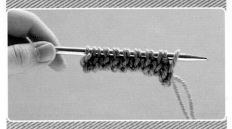

6 Note that you work an even number of rows of the tubular knitting because each row worked is essentially only a half-row knit (you slip half the stitches on each row). The number of rows you work in tubular knit is up to you; more rows means more of a section that is a tube. Then, continue in K1, P1 ribbing.

For K2, P2 Ribbing

Work through the directions to finish the tubular rows. Then, on the next row, you switch stitches to get 2 knits and 2 purls next to each other, as follows.

1 Work the first stitch as it presents (knit or purl).

2 The next stitch is the opposite, so you switch it with the stitch that follows by slipping the next 2 stitches off the left-hand needle and inserting the same needle tip into the first stitch, going in front of the second stitch. Put the second stitch back on the left-hand needle.

3 Work the next stitch on the left-hand needle (it will be the same as the first stitch you worked — knit or purl).

4 The next 3 stitches are in order, but then you must switch stitches again. Continue across the row, switching stitches every 4 stitches.

Möbius Cast On

It only seems fitting to end the cast ons with a technique so unique it stands on its own. A Möbius is a half-twisted loop with only one edge. Many patterns have you knit a rectangle and twist it before sewing the ends or twist the cast-on edge deliberately before knitting. But they are faux Möbiuses and have a full twist in them. The glory and magic of a true Möbius is that it is knit from the center out and has but one edge and a half twist.

Möbius
Cast On

Möbius Cast On

This clever cast on was made popular by the ever-creative Cat Bordhi in her *Treasury of Magical Knitting*. A Möbius makes a wonderfully twisted scarf or shawl, but that is just the beginning. The twist of a Möbius lends itself to all kinds of fantastic shapes, as Cat has shown. The twisted element can be structural or decorative. You knit the piece from the center out, which allows all sorts of play with pattern and color. In structure, the cast on is like a Provisional Cast On (page 110), done over a looped circular needle instead of waste yarn. The cast on has two basic moves and is fairly easy to master, as long as you take care when beginning the first row of knitting.

Extras Circular needle 47–60" long (40" in a pinch); stitch marker

CHARACTERISTICS

- Creates a true Möbius strip
- The need to use long circular needles limits how small the project can be

GOOD FOR

- Bags and baskets with twisted handles
- Möbius wraps, shawls, and scarves

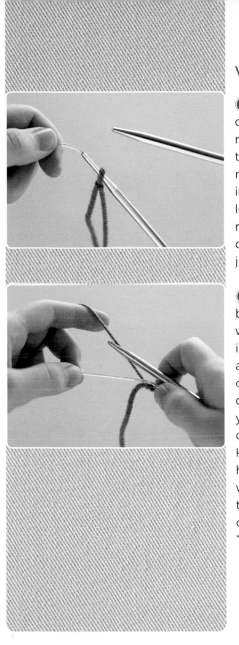

Working the Cast On

1 Holding the needle in a circle, with the tips at the top, make a slip knot with a short tail and place it on the left-hand needle tip. Slide the slip knot into the middle of the cable and let the left-hand tip dangle. The right-hand needle tip does the casting on, and the left-hand tip just hangs and waits.

2 Hold the yarn going to the ball from behind the needle with your left hand (point your index finger up to hold the yarn) and pinch the left side of the cable with the thumb and middle finger of your left hand. The yarn, your hand, and the cable of the circular needle make a kind of triangle. Your right hand holds the right-hand needle tip, while pinching the slip knot with the thumb and middle finger of the right hand. This is the "home" position.

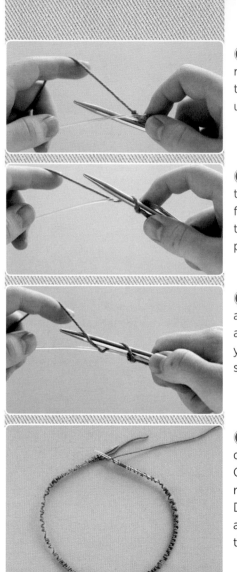

3 Reach the right-hand needle tip in front of the cable, then underneath the cable and up between the cable and yarn.

4 Reach the needle over the top of the yarn and scoop it forward and under the cable, then back up top to the home position.

5 Reach the needle up, over, and behind the yarn and scoop a loop forward. (This looks like a yarnover). Both stitches will be slanting the same way.

6 Repeat steps 3–5 for the desired number of stitches. Count each stitch made by the right-hand needle as 1 stitch. Do not count the stitches that appear on the cable beneath the needle.

Beginning to Knit

7 In order to keep the stitches from twisting, you need to make sure the cable and needles cross only once (making that Möbius twist). To do this, push/ pull the cable, needles, and stitches so that the cable is flat and the sides are parallel to each other. (Cat likens this to a railroad track.) With both needles at the top ready to knit, let the right-hand needle cross the cable at the top. The cable and left-hand needle are parallel to each other all the way around. You may have to rotate the left-hand needle around the cable to make this happen.

8 Place a marker on your right-hand needle and knit the slip knot.

⑨ The stitches on the first half of the round often tend to slide out of order and over each other, so make sure you spread them out as you move them up onto the left-hand needle. Notice, too, that the stitches are mounted alternately. Your job is simply to knit through whatever open triangle presents itself. This means you knit one stitch through the back and the next through the front across the round.

⑩ When you have knit to the point where your stitch marker is hanging on the cable beneath your needle (it cannot be removed at this point), you are halfway around! You'll see your original slip knot again, too. Tug down on it, and knit into the stitch formed by the side of the slip knot.

⑪ Continue knitting (all stitches are now mounted correctly, although they now look as though you've purled them!) until the stitch marker reaches the left-hand needle tip. You have completed the first round. From this point on, knit each round as desired.

Getting It Right

This technique demands a very long circular needle, so the smallest Möbius possible has a circumference of about 20". (That's with a 40" needle, which is extremely tight.) If you want something smaller, felt afterwards!

Part Two

Bind Offs

You've finished the knitting, and all that's left is binding off. You have many options for a happy ending. And, as with cast ons, a little time in the planning (and swatching!) pays off with a finished piece that looks and behaves beautifully. Resist the urge to "just get it done" and invest some energy in determining the best bind off for the characteristics of your project.

It helps to understand the anatomy of stitches in the bind off and see why a particular edge behaves the way it does. Tug on a piece of knitted fabric and note that there is quite a bit of stretch across the width of the fabric, but not so much from top to bottom. This is because the vertical columns of stitches are made up of interlocking loops, like a chain, while a row of stitches is more like a coiled-up spring. When you bind off in the traditional manner, the result is a chain of interlocked stitches like the vertical columns of stitches and

not nearly as elastic as a row of stitches.

A firm bind off is just the ticket in many situations. It keeps things from stretching out of shape; it provides a strong foundation for seams. But what about when you need some stretch in that edge (think the cuff of a toe-up sock or the edge of a lace shawl)? Well, then you've got to switch things up a little. You've got to change the structure of the chain either by making the chains bigger (using a bigger needle or maneuvers, such as knitting through stitches, that increase the size),

Basic *page 146*

Stretchy *page 162*

Decorative *page 178*

Sewn *page 190*

adding more chains (increasing stitches in the bind-off row or row below), or making the chains more elastic (adding extra length in the path of the yarn).

Because of the many different ways to accomplish these variations, like with the cast ons, I have divided the bind offs into categories. The categories relate to function (stretchy or not) or to how they are executed (basic or not). But here's the tricky part: Some bind offs could easily fit into more than one category. For example, the I-Cord Bind Off (page 182) is both stretchy *and* decorative. For further details, always check the characteristics of each technique or look inside the back cover to find bind offs for specific uses.

Basic Bind Offs

The bread-and-butter of bind offs, these basics are the easiest and first learned. They're most likely to be voted "all-purpose" in the yearbook of bind offs.

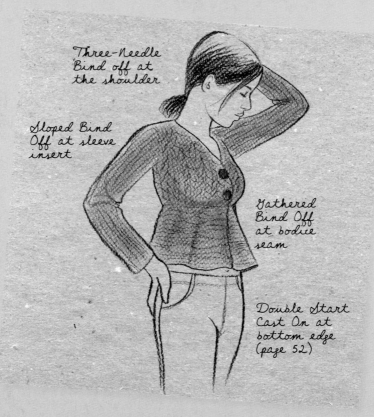

Three-Needle Bind off at the shoulder

Sloped Bind Off at sleeve insert

Gathered Bind Off at bodice seam

Double Start Cast On at bottom edge (page 52)

Traditional
page 148

Slip-Stitch Crochet
page 151

Single Crochet
page 153

Gathered
page 156

Sloped
page 158

Three-Needle
page 160

Traditional Bind Off
a.k.a. Standard, Chain

The Traditional Bind Off is usually the first bind off knitters learn and often the only one they *ever* use. It is easy to learn; works well on knit, purl, and ribbed edges; and looks decent. It can, however, be hard to work loosely enough, requiring many knitters to go up a needle size so the edge does not pull in. The Traditional Bind Off matches the Chained Cast On, so if you have a project where both ends are visible, such as a scarf or afghan, this pair would be a great way to begin and end. This bind off can be worked in any knit-purl stitch pattern. Work each stitch as it presents itself (knit or purl) and bind off according to the directions.

CHARACTERISTICS

- Smooth, attractive edge— looks like chain stitch

GOOD FOR

- Any knit-purl stitch pattern
- Matching Chained Cast On (page 39)

Working the Bind Off

1 Work the first 2 stitches.

2 From the front, insert the left-hand needle tip into the first stitch you made (the one farthest from the needle tip) on the right-hand needle.

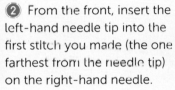

3 Pull it over the second stitch and off the needle.

4 Work the next stitch.

5 Repeat steps 2–4 until you have 1 stitch remaining.

6 Cut the yarn and pull it through last loop.

Slip-Stitch Crochet Bind Off

This is a crocheted version of the Traditional Bind Off, which it resembles exactly. It is less bulky (and tends to be a bit tighter) than the Single Crochet Bind Off (page 153) yet it similarly provides a good base for adding crocheted edgings and trims.

Extras Crochet hook in a size equivalent to the knitting needle size used for project

CHARACTERISTICS

- Firm edge that does not stretch

GOOD FOR

- Adding crochet edgings and fringe
- Matching Chained Cast On (page 39)

Working the Bind Off

1 Insert the crochet hook into the first stitch on the needle, wrap the yarn around, and pull through a loop.

2 Let the stitch fall off the needle.

3 Insert the hook into the next stitch on the needle and wrap the yarn around. Pull the loop through the stitch, again letting the stitch fall off the left-hand needle. Finally (as is just about to happen in this picture), pull the yarn through the loop on the crochet hook.

4 Repeat step 3 until you have 1 stitch remaining. Cut the yarn and pull it through the last loop on the hook.

Single Crochet Bind Off

Crochet bind offs are especially useful in dealing with nonelastic yarns, such as cottons and silks, as they create a firm edge that does not stretch out. A crochet bind off also provides a great foundation for adding crocheted edgings and trims.

Extras Crochet hook in a size equivalent to the knitting needle size used for project

CHARACTERISTICS

- Firm edge that does not stretch

GOOD FOR

- Adding crochet edgings and fringe
- Matching Chained Cast On (page 39)

Working the Bind Off

① Insert the hook into the first stitch on the needle knitwise, catch the working yarn with the hook, and pull through a loop.

② Let the stitch fall off the needle.

③ Insert the hook into the next stitch, wrap, and pull through a loop, letting the stitch fall off the needle. You now have 2 loops on the crochet hook.

④ Wrap the yarn around the hook.

5 Pull it through the 2 loops on the hook.

6 Repeat steps 3–5 until you have 1 stitch remaining. Cut the tail and pull it through the remaining loop on the hook.

Gathered Bind Off
a.k.a. One-over-Two

The Gathered Bind Off pulls the stitches together along the bound-off edge. This is useful for stitch patterns that tend to spread a lot, such as cables or openwork. You can combine it with a Traditional Bind Off (page 148), using the Gathered Bind Off only in the areas that need to be pulled in.

CHARACTERISTICS

- Pulls edge in

GOOD FOR

- Preventing flaring along the edge of stitch patterns with a lot of lateral spread

Getting It Right

Use larger needles to prevent the edge from becoming too tight.

Working the Bind Off

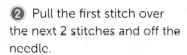

1 Work the first 3 stitches.

2 Pull the first stitch over the next 2 stitches and off the needle.

3 Work 1 more stitch.

4 Repeat steps 2 and 3 until you have 2 stitches remaining on the right needle. Bind off the last 2 stitches by pulling the first over the second and then cutting the yarn and pulling it through the last stitch.

Sloped Bind Off

The Sloped Bind Off is a great way to smooth out the stair-step effect of multiple bind offs on a neck or shoulder edge. You will still be working the bind off in steps, but by not working the final stitch in the row before you bind off, it softens the jagged effect. Plus, it is simpler than short rows (which involve wrapping and turning, and then picking up the wraps again), and it creates an even edge for seaming. But you will not be able to seam it with the Three-Needle Bind Off (page 160) because the stitches are bound off in steps.

CHARACTERISTICS

- Turns stair-step bind offs into a slope
- Smooth edge for seaming

GOOD FOR

- Armholes, sleeves, and shoulders
- Neck openings

Working the Bind Off

① On the row before the first bind-off row, work up to the last stitch in the row. Do not work this stitch; leave it on the left-hand needle and turn the work.

② Slip the first stitch purlwise. Now you have 2 stitches on the right-hand needle.

③ Pass the unworked stitch over the slipped stitch.

④ Continue working (knitting or purling) and binding off the required number of stitches, then finish working across the row

⑤ On the row before your next bind-off row, once again, do not work the final stitch. Leave it on the left-hand needle, turn work, and continue with steps 2–4.

Three-Needle Bind Off
a.k.a. Seam

The Three-Needle Bind Off is a method of joining, or seaming, two pieces of knitting and binding off simultaneously. It is commonly used to join the shoulder seams of sweaters, where it lines up the stitches on the front and back beautifully. The edge is smooth and invisible when bound off with right sides together, or it can form a decorative ridge when bound off with wrong sides together. The seam it creates is pretty stable, but if you are joining particularly long pieces or if you are worried about stretching, you probably should bind off the edges separately and sew the seam by hand.

Extras Third needle the same size as used for the project

CHARACTERISTICS

- Firm edge
- Binds off and seams simultaneously

GOOD FOR

- Shoulder seams
- Any relatively short seams

Getting It Right

Working with three needles can feel awkward at first. I find it easiest to hold the two needles with stitches in my left hand as if they were one needle and the needle I am knitting with in my right hand.

Working the Bind Off

When you are ready to bind off, move both sets of stitches from holders back onto needles, being sure to orient the stitches so that the first ones to be worked are at the needle tips.

1 With right sides of the work facing, hold the two needles together. Each piece should have the same number of stitches. With a third needle, knit together 1 stitch from the front needle and 1 stitch from the back needle.

2 Knit the next stitch on each needle together.

3 Bind off in the traditional manner, pulling the first stitch over the second stitch on the right-hand needle.

4 Repeat steps 2 and 3 across the row until 1 stitch remains. Cut the yarn and pull it through the last stitch.

Stretchy Bind Offs

Sometimes you want your bound-off edge to have some flexibility. Sometimes you want it to be quite elastic, as in the cuff of a sock or the edge of a lace piece that will be stretched to reveal the lace pattern. These are the bind offs for those situations. The techniques vary in how they achieve this and the degree of stretch that they add; be sure to consult the characteristics lists for those details. These are not the only bind offs that create an elastic edge — many of the sewn and decorative bind offs are also stretchy, so flip to the inside back cover to find other stretchy bind offs.

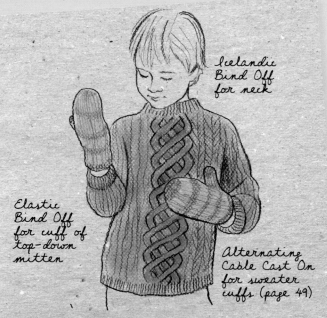

Icelandic Bind Off for neck

Elastic Bind Off for cuff of top-down mitten

Alternating Cable Cast On for sweater cuffs (page 49)

Getting It Right

For ribbed edges, like the top of a sock, you can bind off in pattern. Work each individual stitch as it presents itself — knit or purl. When working two together, work it either knit or purl, based on the second stitch of the pair.

Yarnover Bind Off

The Yarnover Bind Off adds an extra loop between stitches in the bind-off row. This makes for a very stretchy edge, which can be a good thing if that's what you're after. For instance, it would be great for binding off the edge of a lace shawl where you're really stretching it out to open up the lace. The downside is that it flares the edge, which can be pretty unattractive if you're not blocking it.

CHARACTERISTICS

- Very stretchy edge
- Edge flares

GOOD FOR

- Lace
- Ruffles and flares

Working the Bind Off

1 Knit the first 2 stitches. Pull the first stitch over the second, as in a Traditional Bind Off (page 148).

2 Wrap the yarn around the right-hand needle (yarnover).

3 Pull the first stitch over the yarnover.

4 Knit the next stitch and bind off 1 stitch.

5 Repeat steps 2–4 until 1 stitch remains. Cut the yarn and pull it through the last stitch.

Suspended Bind Off

This bind off is very similar to the Traditional Bind Off (page 148) yet more elastic, making it useful for edges that require more stretch. It is also good for knitters who have a hard time binding off loosely. Instead of increasing needle size in the traditional knitted bind off to prevent a too-tight edge, try using this Suspended Bind Off — so-called because, as you see in step 2, you don't drop the stitch from the needle as quickly as in the Traditional Bind Off.

CHARACTERISTICS

- Elastic edge

GOOD FOR

- Knitters who bind off too tightly

Working the Bind Off

1 Knit the first 2 stitches.

2 Use the left-hand needle to pull the first stitch over the second stitch, but do not drop the stitch from the left-hand needle.

3 Reach over in front of that stitch you've just put back on the left-hand needle . . .

and knit the next stitch on the left-hand needle.

4 Drop both stitches off the left-hand needle. You now have 2 stitches on your right-hand needle.

5 Repeat steps 2–4 until 1 stitch remains. Cut the yarn and pull it through the last stitch.

Lace Bind Off
a.k.a. Russian, Purl Two Together

The Lace Bind Off creates a stretchy edge that is suitable for necks, sleeve cuffs, and sock tops. It also works well, as the name suggests, for lace pieces where you want a lot of stretch to accommodate the openness of the lace pattern.

CHARACTERISTICS

- Flexible edge

GOOD FOR

- Lace
- Necks
- Cuffs of socks
- Top-down mittens or hats

Working the Bind Off

① Knit the first 2 stitches together through the back loops.

② Slip the stitch on the right-hand needle back to the left-hand needle purlwise.

③ Repeat steps 1 and 2 until you have 1 stitch left. Cut the yarn and pull it tightly through the last stitch.

Getting It Right

- Knitting through the front of the stitches makes a slightly different look.

- You can also work this in purl. You may find the purl version to be slightly faster.

Try swatching with these different variations to see which looks best with your project.

Elastic Bind Off

This is a variation on the Lace Bind Off (page 168). The effect is very similar and it creates an elastic edge that is good for lace, sock tops, necks, and cuffs.

CHARACTERISTICS

- Elastic edge, a bit stretchier than the Lace Bind Off

GOOD FOR

- Lace
- Stretchy necks
- Cuffs of socks
- Top-down mittens or hats

Working the Bind Off

1. Work the first 2 stitches.

2. Slip the stitches purlwise back to the left-hand needle.

3. Work these 2 stitches together through the back loops.

4. Work the next stitch.

5. Repeat steps 2–4 until 2 stitches remain. Knit those stitches together through the back loops. Cut the yarn and pull it through the last loop.

Icelandic Bind Off

This bind off creates a very flexible, neat edge. It is commonly used for lace projects where you want a lot of stretch to open up the lace patterns when blocking. It is a little trickier to work than the Lace or Elastic bind offs; try it to see if the resultant edge is worth the effort for your project.

CHARACTERISTICS

- Elastic edge

GOOD FOR

- Lace
- Rolled necklines

Working the Bind Off

1 Knit the first stitch.

2 Slip the stitch purlwise back to the left-hand needle.

3 Insert the right-hand needle tip through the first stitch purlwise, and then into the second stitches ready to knit.

4 Pulling the new stitch through both stitches, let both stitches on the left-hand needle drop off.

5 Repeat steps 2–4 until 1 stitch remains. Cut the yarn and pull it through the last loop.

Jeny's Surprisingly Stretchy Bind Off

This brilliant bind off is the brainchild of Jeny Staiman, who generously allowed me to share it here. It is simple to execute, yet it adds a degree of stretchiness not found in other knitted bind offs. Because it is not sewn, it is easier to work over long stretches of fabric. And it works for any stitch pattern: K1, P1 rib; K2, P2 rib; or whatever combinations you come up with. The edge folds along the ribbed stitches like an accordion, stretching out an amazing amount and then snapping back in, making it perfect for toe-up socks. It is also great for hats, neck edges, and top-down mittens and gloves.

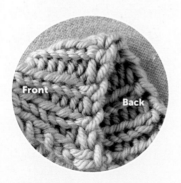

CHARACTERISTICS

- Very stretchy
- Easy to work over long edges

GOOD FOR

- Any ribbing patterns
- Toe-up socks
- Top-down mittens and hats

Processing the Stitches

Note: To work this bind off, which is basically a Traditional Bind Off (page 148) with yarn-overs thrown in, you "process" each stitch in a particular way, depending on whether it is a knit or purl.

Processing a Knit Stitch

* Wrap the yarn around the right-hand needle over the top, around the front, and back to the back. This is a reverse yarnover.

* Knit 1 stitch.

* Pull the yarnover over the knit stitch.

Processing a Purl Stitch

- Make a yarnover, this time going from front around the back and ending with the yarn in front.

- Purl 1 stitch.

- Pull the yarnover over the purl stitch.

Working the Bind Off

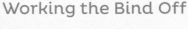

1 Process each of the first 2 stitches as described. You now have 2 stitches on your right-hand needle. Pull the right-hand stitch over the left-hand stitch and off the needle.

2 Process the next stitch, knit or purl, as needed.

3 Again, pull the right-hand stitch over the left-hand stitch and off the needle.

4 Repeat steps 2 and 3 until 1 stitch remains. Cut the yarn and pull it through the last stitch.

Note: Once you have processed the first stitch, on all remaining stitches you can pull the yarn-over and the processed stitch off the needle together in one step.

Getting It Right

The trick with this bind off is to remember which way to do the yarnover. For knitting, you start at the back and end at the back for your yarnover. For purling, you do the reverse: Start the yarn in front and wrap it around, ending in the front again.

Decorative
Bind Offs

The techniques in this section add a decorative effect to the bound-off edge. Usually reserved for edges that will not be seamed, they add a beautiful finishing touch. The picot bind offs in particular are quite elastic, which makes them popular choices at the tops of socks and the necks of baby garments. All these bind offs are as functional as they are decorative.

Two-Row Bind Off at fringe

Two-Row

I-Cord

Picot 1

Picot 2

Two-Row Bind Off

This bind off creates a subtle row of eyelets along the edge, which makes it great for afghans, shawls, and scarves that you want to attach fringe to after finishing. It tends to pull in a little on stockinette fabric, though this can be blocked out. On ribbing it looks great.

CHARACTERISTICS

- Very neat edge
- Edge has row of tiny eyelets

GOOD FOR

- Ribbing
- Adding fringe
- Afghans, shawls, and scarves

Working the Bind Off

① Knit 1 stitch, purl 1 stitch.

② Pull the knit stitch over the purl stitch, binding it off.

③ Repeat steps 1 and 2 across the row, which leaves all purl stitches on the needle.

④ Turn the work and slip the first 2 stitches purlwise. Pull the first stitch over the second stitch, binding it off.

⑤ Slip the next stitch purlwise and pull the first stitch over this stitch. Repeat across the row until 1 stitch remains. Sew this stitch down to the knitting.

I-Cord Bind Off

The I-Cord Bind Off creates an I-cord band along the bind-off edge. This makes an attractive, flexible edging for necks, cuffs, pocket openings, and other places where you want something simple yet finished. If you are not a crocheter, substitute an I-Cord Bind Off for edges that call for a crochet trim.

CHARACTERISTICS

- Attractive, substantial edge
- Elastic edge
- Uses more yarn than most other bind offs
- Three-dimensional, rounded edge

GOOD FOR

- Necklines or places that will be stretched
- Instead of a crocheted edge
- Making with a contrasting color

Working the Bind Off

1 With right side facing, cast on 3 stitches using the Knitted Cast On (page 31).

2 Knit the first 2 stitches.

3 Knit 2 together (the last stitch of the I-cord and the first stitch of the knitted piece) through the back loops.

4 Slip these 3 stitches back to the left-hand needle purlwise. (Slipping purlwise ensures that you don't twist the stitches.)

⑤ Repeat steps 2–4 until 3 stitches remain.

⑥ Bind off the remaining stitches using the Traditional Bind Off (page 148).

Getting It Right

- You can use only 2 stitches for a very small I-cord or 4–6 stitches for a bigger I-cord.

- You can work this in reverse stockinette as well; simply purl the added stitches instead of knitting them. This version looks especially good with garter stitch garments.

Picot 1 Bind Off

The Picot 1 Bind Off creates a delicate, decorative edge for pieces that will not be seamed. It looks beautiful on the edges of scarves and afghans, and many people love it for edging baby garments. It adds elasticity to the edge, making it well-suited for lacework. This method of working a picot edge is simple and flexible — you can vary the size of the picot and the distance between picots simply by changing the number of extra stitches cast on and the number of stitches bound off in between each picot.

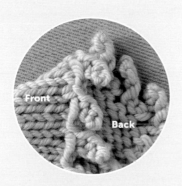

CHARACTERISTICS

- Decorative edge
- Elastic edge
- Uses more yarn than most other bind offs

GOOD FOR

- Edges of lace shawls, cuffs, and hats
- Matching Picot Cast On (page 70)
- Baby garments

Working the Bind Off

1 Knit the first 2 stitches and bind off 1 using the Traditional Bind Off (page 148).

2 Transfer the remaining stitch from the right-hand needle to the left-hand needle and use the Knitted Cast On (page 31) to cast on 3 stitches.

3 Bind off 5 stitches. (These are the 3 stitches just cast on, the 1 you worked in step 1 and transferred back to the left needle, and 1 more.)

4 Repeat steps 2 and 3 until one stitch remains.

5 Cut the yarn and pull it through the last stitch.

Getting It Right

Picots can be spaced farther apart by binding off more stitches between the cast-on stitches. Take care not to place them too close together, or the edge may ripple or flare.

Picot 2 Bind Off

Here is another way to do a Picot Bind Off. It also creates a decorative scalloped edge, though the picot is a bit more understated. It is more fiddly than Picot 1 Bind Off because it involves turning rows twice for each picot. Try both to see which version produces the effect you are looking for.

CHARACTERISTICS

- Decorative edge
- Elastic edge
- Uses more yarn than most other bind offs

GOOD FOR

- Edges of lace shawls, cuffs, and hats
- Baby garments

Working the Bind Off

1 Knit the first 2 stitches and then bind off 1 using the Traditional Bind Off (page 148).

2 Turn your work and use the Knitted Cast On (page 31) to cast on 3 more stitches. (You now have 4 stitches on this needle.)

3 Turn your work again and use the left-hand needle to pull the second, third, and fourth stitches over the first stitch.

4 Bind off 2 stitches using the Traditional Bind Off.

5 Repeat steps 2–4 until one stitch remains. Cut the yarn and pull it through the last stitch.

Sewn Bind Offs

These types of bind offs are accomplished by sewing the edge with a piece of yarn threaded through a blunt tapestry needle. In general, many of these bind offs create very elastic edges. There are, however, a few drawbacks to working a sewn bind off. Because the seaming yarn is being pulled through every stitch, often multiple times, the yarn can become frayed and tangled, especially over long edges. You also need to be careful not to split the yarn with the tapestry needle. And if you ever need to undo the edge, say to add length, it is slow and laborious. Maintaining consistent tension may also prove challenging. The added flexibility of these edges, however, may make sewn bind offs worth these challenges.

Tubular Bind Off for top-down hat

Kitchener Stitch Bind Off at toe of sock

Slip Knot Cast On for sock cuffs (page 59)

Kitchener Stitch

Sewn

Invisible Ribbed

Tubular

Interlock

Kitchener Stitch

The infamous Kitchener Stitch is a way of binding off, or grafting, two sets of stitches. Most frequently this is done on the toe of a sock, though it can be done to graft stitches together in other situations, such as joining two halves of a scarf together or as the final step in a tubular bind off. You need to have an equal number of stitches on each of the two needles.

Extras Blunt tapestry needle

CHARACTERISTICS

- Invisible edge
- Grafts two sets of stitches

GOOD FOR

- Finishing the toes of socks
- Joining any two pieces with the same number of stitches

Working the Bind Off

1 Hold both needles together so that the wrong sides are together and the right sides of the work are facing outward. The yarn tail should be on the right side; thread it through a tapestry needle.

2 Insert the tapestry needle through the first stitch on the front needle as if to purl and pull the yarn through. Leave the stitch on the needle.

3 Insert the tapestry needle through the first stitch on the back needle as if to knit and pull the yarn through. Leave the stitch on the needle.

4 On the front needle, insert the tapestry needle through the first stitch knitwise and slip the stitch off the needle.

⑤ Insert the tapestry needle through the next stitch purlwise and leave it on the needle.

⑥ On the back needle, insert the tapestry needle through the first stitch purlwise and slip the stitch off the needle.

⑦ Insert the tapestry needle through the next stitch knitwise and leave the stitch on the needle.

⑧ Repeat steps 4–7 until all stitches have been worked. You will have 1 stitch left on the back needle; go through with the thread purlwise and weave the end in.

Sewn Bind Off

The Sewn Bind Off was a favorite of Elizabeth Zimmermann.
It forms a very elastic edging that is useful for edges that are
subjected to stretching, such as necklines and cuffs. In appearance it forms a ridge much like a purl row.

Extras Blunt tapestry needle

CHARACTERISTICS

- Elastic, slightly ridged edge

GOOD FOR

- Necks
- Cuffs

Working the Bind Off

1 Measure out a tail of yarn that is three times the width of the knitting to be bound off. Thread this onto a blunt tapestry needle. Work from right to left with the right side facing you.

2 Insert the tapestry needle purlwise through the first 2 stitches on the needle and pull the yarn through. Leave the stitches on the needle.

3 Insert the tapestry needle knitwise through the first stitch on the needle and drop this stitch off the needle.

4 Repeat steps 2 and 3. You will end with 1 stitch left on the needle; insert the tapestry needle through this stitch purlwise, drop the stitch from the needle, and weave the end in.

Invisible Ribbed Bind Off

a.k.a. Knit-One Purl-One

This sewn bind off creates a very elastic edge on ribbing. The edge is, as the name implies, nearly invisible, and the flexibility produced makes it ideal for necks, cuffs, and toe-up socks.

Extras Blunt tapestry needle

Getting It Right

As you're sewing, keep in mind that each stitch is worked twice: first with its opposite move (through a knit stitch purlwise) and next by sliding it off the needle with its matching maneuver (a knit stitch coming off as the tapestry needle goes through it knitwise).

CHARACTERISTICS

- Invisible edge
- Very stretchy

GOOD FOR

- Necks
- Cuffs
- Toe-up socks

Working the Bind Off

1 Measure out a tail of yarn three times the width of the knitting to be bound off and thread it on a tapestry needle. You will be working from right to left, with the right side facing you.

2 Insert the tapestry needle from right to left (purlwise) through the first (knit) stitch on the needle and pull through.

3 Insert the tapestry needle knitwise through the next (purl) stitch and pull the yarn through.

4 Insert the tapestry needle knitwise into the first knit stitch and pull the yarn through, letting the stitch fall off the needle.

5 Insert the tapestry needle purlwise into the next knit stitch and pull the yarn through.

6 Insert the tapestry needle purlwise into the first purl stitch and pull the yarn through, letting the stitch fall from the needle.

7 Bring the tapestry needle behind the first knit stitch and insert it knitwise into the next purl stitch, pulling the yarn through.

8 Repeat steps 4–7 until 1 stitch remains Pull the tail through the last stitch and weave in the end.

Tubular Bind Off

The Tubular Bind Off creates an edge that is identical to the Provisional Tubular Cast On and the Italian Tubular Cast On. The edge is very stretchy, elastic, and smooth in appearance. There is, in fact, no real "edge" to be seen — the rib stitches seem to just roll over the edge. This makes a great way to finish pieces subjected to a lot of stretching, such as cuffs, turtlenecks, sock tops, and hat brims. And it's ideal for those situations where you want the cast on and bind off to mirror each other exactly. It is worked on a K1, P1 ribbing. You begin this bind off two rows before you want your piece to actually end.

Extras Blunt tapestry needle; two double-point or circular needles, one or two sizes smaller than those used for the rest of the piece (for ease only; they won't affect size)

CHARACTERISTICS

- Invisible, rolled edge
- Elastic edge

GOOD FOR

- Matching Provisional Tubular Cast On (page 123) and Italian Tubular Cast On (page 132)
- Turtlenecks
- Cuffs
- Toe-up socks

Working the Bind Off

Note: These directions are for binding off in rows on a flat piece.

1 Work K1, P1 ribbing to 2 rows less than the desired length.

2 Knit each knit stitch and slip each purl stitch, with yarn in front.

Repeat step 2 for 3 more rows.

3 Hold the two empty double-point or circular needles in your right hand and your knitting in your left hand. In this step, you separate the knit and purl stitches. To do so, transfer the stitches, one at a time, to the new needles, alternating knit and purl stitches, with the knit going to the front needle and the purl going to the back needle. Slip all stitches purlwise.

4 Graft stitches together using the Kitchener stitch (page 192).

Interlock Bind Off

This is another great invention from Jeny Staiman, creator of Jeny's Surprisingly Stretchy Bind Off (page 174), who was looking for a stretchy, invisible bind off. This sewn bind off can be worked in stockinette or ribbing. The edge is indeed very elastic and snaps back into shape without ruffling. In addition, it blends into the fabric almost invisibly. When worked over stockinette stitch, it is an exact match for the Backward Loop Cast On, which makes it great for scarves, fingerless gloves, and other projects where you want matching edges.

Extras Blunt tapestry needle

CHARACTERISTICS

- Very elastic
- Invisible edge

GOOD FOR

- Matching Backward Loop Cast On (page 20) when worked in stockinette
- Fingerless gloves
- Scarves
- Stretchy ribbing

Preparing to Bind Off

Cut a tail of yarn four to five times the length of the edge to be bound off. Thread the yarn on a blunt tapestry needle.

Note: If working in the round, start with Setup (below). If working flat, go directly to Working the Bind Off (next page), in either stockinette or K1, P1 rib (page 205).

Setup for Working in the Round

- Insert the tapestry needle through the first stitch on the left-hand needle purlwise and pull the yarn through, leaving the stitch on the needle.

- Insert the tapestry needle through the last stitch on the right-hand needle knitwise and pull the yarn through, leaving the stitch on the needle.

Working the Bind Off in Stockinette

1 Insert the tapestry needle through the first stitch on the left-hand needle knitwise and drop the first stitch off the knitting needle.

2 Take the tapestry needle through the second stitch purlwise.

3 Pull the yarn through, leaving a loop before the first stitch (the one just dropped).

4 Bring the tapestry needle through the loop, front to back, making sure the loop is not twisted.

5 Snug gently by pulling the tapestry needle horizontally to the right.

6 Repeat steps 1–5 until all stitches are bound off.

If working in the round, insert the tapestry needle through the very first loop you made, just after the setup, from front to back. Snug gently, then weave in the tail.

Working the Bind Off in K1, P1 Rib

Start with a knit stitch at the tip of your left needle.

1 Insert the tapestry needle knitwise through the first 2 stitches on the left-hand needle, dropping the first stitch.

2 Pull the yarn, leaving a loop before the first stitch (the one just dropped).

3 Bring the tapestry needle from back to front through the loop of yarn, making sure the loop is not twisted.

4 Snug gently by pulling the tapestry needle horizontally to the right.

5 Insert tapestry needle through the next 2 stitches on the left-hand needle purlwise and drop the first stitch from the needle.

6 Pull the yarn, leaving a loop before the first stitch (the one just dropped).

7 Bring the tapestry needle from the front to the back through the loop of yarn, making sure the loop is not twisted.

8 Snug gently by pulling the tapestry needle horizontally to the right.

9 Repeat steps 1–8 until all stitches are bound off, binding off last two stitches together. If working in the round, end with steps 1 and 2. Then take the tapestry needle through the very first loop you made, just after the setup, from front to back. Snug gently, then weave in the tail.

Getting It Right for K1, P1 Ribbing

- If the first stitch is a knit stitch, go through the first 2 stitches knitwise. The yarn goes to the back; bring the tapestry needle through the loop from back to front.

- If the first stitch is a purl, go through the first 2 stitches purlwise. The yarn comes to the front; bring the tapestry needle through the loop from front to back.

RESOURCES

Reading List

Bordhi, Cat. *A Treasury of Magical Knitting*. Passing Paws Press, 2004.

Editors of *Vogue Knitting* Magazine. *Vogue Knitting: The Ultimate Knitting Book*. Sixth & Spring, 2002.

Hiatt, June Hemmons. *The Principles of Knitting*, rev. ed. Touchstone, 2012.

Johnson, Wendy D. *Socks from the Toe Up: Essential Techniques and Patterns from Wendy Knits*. Potter Craft, 2009.

Square, Vicki. *The Knitter's Companion*, rev. ed. Interweave Press, 2006.

Stanley, Montse. *Reader's Digest Knitter's Handbook*. Reader's Digest, 1993.

Stoller, Debbie. *Stitch 'n Bitch Superstar Knitting*. Workman Publishing, 2010.

Turner, Sharon. *Teach Yourself Visually: Knitting*, 2nd ed. Wiley Publishing, 2010.

Online Resources

Jeny's Stretchy Slipknot Cast-On
YouTube
www.youtube.com/
watch?v=3n8E3I6Cg2k
Jeny Staiman demonstrates the Slip Knot Cast On

Jeny's Surprisingly Stretchy Bind-Off
Personal Footprints by Cat Bordhi, YouTube
www.youtube.com/
watch?v=abBhe-JYmgI
Cat Bordhi demonstrates Jeny's Surprisingly Stretchy Bind Off

Judy's Magic Cast On
YouTube
www.youtube.com/
watch?v=1pmxRDZ-cwo
www.beyondtoes.com
Demonstrates Judy Becker's cast on

Knitting Daily
Interweave Press, LLC
www.knittingdaily.com
Posts and instructional videos

KnittingHelp.com
www.knittinghelp.com
Videos of cast-on and bind-off techniques

Knitty Magazine
www.knitty.com
Articles about cast-on and bind-off techniques

The Moebius Cast-On
Intro to Moebius Knitting, YouTube
www.youtube.com/
watch?v=LVnTda7F2V4
Cat Bordhi demonstrates the Möbius Cast On

Very Stretchy Cast-On for Double and Single Ribbing
YouTube
www.youtube.com/
watch?v=wf8cY_djTRI
Tillybuddy demonstrates her stretchy cast on

ACKNOWLEDGMENTS

THE JOURNEY TO THIS BOOK has involved help from many sources along the way. Finding a way to acknowledge all of them is daunting, to say the least. My own knitting began with my mother, and I owe her a great deal for introducing me to fiber and creativity. Her patience in teaching allowed me to develop my skills and confidence. Learning to work with my hands is a gift she gave me that blesses me every day. When I announced that I wanted to support myself with my knitting, she promptly went out and bought me a library of books to help me develop my skills. Her enthusiastic support of my creativity encouraged my development as a craftsperson. My work as a fiber artist is a testament to the foundation she gave me, and I am filled with gratitude and love for her.

In my exploration of knitting over the years I have been influenced and educated by the contributions of June Hiatt, Montse Stanley, Barbara Walker, and Elizabeth Zimmermann, among others. Their work helped me to understand the structure of knitting so that I can create what I see in my mind's eye. Thanks as well to those creative individuals who have found new ways to cast on and bind off and have allowed me to share them in this book: Judy Becker, Jane Pimlott, and Cat Bordhi. Special thanks to Jeny Staiman, who not only contributed two bind offs, but helped me greatly in explaining how bind offs work. I appreciate her openness and enthusiastic support: It was a huge help to have another technique geek to talk through ideas with.

I have the great good fortune to work in a yarn store, surrounded not only by beautiful fibers, but also by inspiring and creative people — staff and customers alike. Many thanks to my colleagues and friends at WEBS for their encouragement and support of my work on this book. Thank you to Kathy and Steve Elkins for believing in me and giving me new challenges to work with; to my friend and mentor Pixie Benoist, who planted the seed when she asked me to teach a class on cast ons and bind offs; to Gail Callahan, whose sage advice as an author helped me navigate the writing process; to Dori Betjemann, for being the very first person I went to for help sorting out the differences between techniques and providing a wealth of knitting expertise; to my students who helped me refine these instructions; and to those I work with every day — thanks for the kind words, advice, and inspiration.

Thanks to the many knitters who helped me by "test driving" my instructions: Janice Watkins, Moe Belliveau, Gail Callahan, Greta Shaver, Dolly Hurd, and Suzette Alsop-Jones. Their feedback helped me to clarify and shape this book.

Thanks to the crew at Storey: to Gwen Steege for taking a chance on me and guiding me through the process; to my editor, Pam Thompson, for helping me turn a stack of instructions into a well-crafted book. Her insightful suggestions and knitting expertise helped create a book that was much more than I initially imagined it could be (not to mention her above-and-beyond swatch-knitting help!). Thanks, too, to Kathy Brock, whose sharp eye helped keep the book clear and consistent; to photographer John Polak and model Heather Minott, whose patience and precision captured in pictures what I tried to explain in words; and to Mary Velgos, for turning what seemed to me like a dry textbook into a beautiful and engaging book.

Thanks to friends and family: to my friend Crane Cesario for listening to me question myself and reminding me that I don't have to know everything to be a good teacher; and to my friend Nina Dayton for showing me (more than once!) the Double-Twist Loop Cast On. My family is my foundation, and I am forever grateful for their love and support. Thanks especially to my dad, Charles Bestor, and sister, Jenner Bestor, for keeping the home fires burning brightly throughout the writing of this book, for countless hours of child care and many good suppers, for support and encouragement above and beyond. And thanks to my darling daughter, Cady, for giving me the space to write and for your overflowing creativity and the ways you encourage me to believe in myself. I love you!

INDEX

Other Storey Titles You Will Enjoy

2-at-a-Time Socks, by Melissa Morgan-Oakes.
An easy-to-learn new technique to banish Second Sock
Syndrome forever!
144 pages. Hardcover with concealed wire-o.
ISBN 978-1-58017-691-0.

Circular Knitting Workshop, by Margaret Radcliffe.
Detailed photographic sequences for every classic technique
on circular knitting needles, plus 35 demonstration projects.
320 pages. Paper. ISBN 978-1-60342-999-3.

The Essential Guide to Color Knitting Techniques,
by Margaret Radcliffe.
Stripes, stranded knitting, intarsia and more multicolor knitting
methods, clearly explained with step-by-step photographs.
320 pages. Hardcover with jacket. ISBN 978-1-60342-0402.

The Knitter's Life List, by Gwen W. Steege.
A road map to a lifetime of knitting challenges and adventures.
320 pages. Paper with flaps. ISBN 978-1-60342-996-2.

The Knitting Answer Book, by Margaret Radcliffe.
Answers for every knitting quandry — an indispensable addition
to every knitter's project bag.
400 pages. Flexibind. ISBN 978-1-58017-599-9.

Sock Yarn One-Skein Wonders, edited by Judith Durant.
One-of-a-kind patterns for baby clothes, mittens, scarves, hats,
bags, and of course, socks!
288 pages. Paper. ISBN 978-1-60342-579-7.

These and other books from Storey Publishing are available
wherever quality books are sold or by calling 1-800-441-5700.
Visit us at *www.storey.com*.